RUNNING OUT OF TIME

A Critical Review of Evolution, Creation and Consummation

Graham Wilson

Graham Wilson
15 March 1995

Foreword by Geoffrey Grogan

The Rowans Press

ISBN 0952 488 40X

Published by
The Rowans Press
8 The Rowans,
Gullane,
East Lothian
EH31 2DU

Printed and bound in Great Britain by
Cox & Wyman Ltd, Reading, Berkshire

Cover design by Donna Macleod

Contents

Foreword

Missionaries working in Africa say that African preachers usually have a way of preaching the gospel which is significantly different from the way it is normally preached in Britain and other western countries today. Like western preachers, of course, they focus on the Lord Jesus Christ and on His cross and Resurrection. What is distinctive about them however is that they nearly always set Christ and His work in a very broad context, for they start with the Creation and they end with the Consummation.

Graham Wilson too deals with the way things began and the way they will end. The Bible handles both issues, but they are of interest to more than Christians. Not to be concerned at all about where we came from or where we are going to is to be a most unthinking person.

He holds to creation rather than evolution, to recent creation rather than ancient creation, to a universal as distinct from a local flood, and he maintains that the Bible does not teach millennialism nor a dispensational scheme.

All this means, not only that most non-Christians will find him cutting across their ideas but that this will apply to many Christians too. I find it good to read books that stimulate me to think in new ways, and this book will do that for most of its readers, even though, as I think he suspects, not too many will agree with him on every point. He and I have known each other for some years and it is good to see him now putting his thoughts on paper, and not just in 'Letters to the Editor'!

Mr Wilson has written an untechnical book, unencumbered for the most part by the language of the specialist scientist or professional theologian. His style is direct and, at times, blunt, but there are also touches of humour. It is 'a good read', and I hope many will buy it and read it.

Rev Geoffrey Grogan
Principal Emeritus of the Glasgow Bible College
(formerly known as the Bible Training Institute)

Preface

Many years ago I stated (or threatened) that I was going to write a book on a particular biblical theme ! Having been born and bred in Belfast and having moved in Baptist circles, it would not be too difficult to guess the subject - yes, the Return of Jesus Christ, or as better known, the Second Advent or Consummation.

In my experience in the fifties and sixties, there was only one viewpoint proclaimed and therefore this found widespread acceptance - the 'two-stage' Return of Christ, popularised by the 'Scofield Bible'. Most of us were unaware that there were other approaches dealing with this vital topic. Once I discovered and considered them, it was clear that a book had to be written.

Intertwined with this theme of the Second Coming was the matter of the nation of Israel and especially its possible future role. Here was a nation, called and blessed by God, that had existed for almost four thousand years and still awaited its Messiah. It was inconceivable that such a subject could be omitted from any proposed book.

Over the years the topic of the origins or genesis of things also claimed a certain level of priority. Indeed it is difficult to consider, from scripture, the consummation without having due regard for the commencement. I believed that God created everything in the beginning and, as 'Science' (not basic applied science), claimed that the earth was billions of years old, who was I to argue ! Clearly I had some difficulty with aspects of Genesis chapters 1 and 2 because Adam and Eve were to be dated only thousands or possibly a few tens of thousands and not millions of years ago.

The concept of evolution gave some cause for thought. Was it factual or was it really a belief, indeed akin to a sort of religion ? Could it genuinely cope with the issues and mysteries of life and death, goodwill and evil, faith and suffering which are the common lot of humanity ?

Various events over the past three years forced me back, with fresh eyes, to the bible and, in particular, to Genesis and it was therefore inevitable that this topic would also be included in any book.The Almighty seemed to reveal himself as the God of discrete actions rather than gradualistic processes and this matter called for inspection.

I am the first to admit that it is very difficult to do justice to these major themes in one book. Basically I have, as a layman, written for laypeople. I have sought to draw attention to key matters and I have also suggested some books for further reading.

To a large extent, I have refrained from making specific quotations other than from the scriptures. Arguably, references may be appropriate in various paragraphs but, from experience, these can tend to be frustrating unless given in considerable detail. It can be intimidating to quote certain authors to the exclusion of others who perhaps adopt a somewhat different stance. In the final analysis, readers must weigh up all the available evidence, through study and consultation, in order to arrive at their own viewpoints. For the Christian, however, such convictions must be compatible with the breadth of the teaching of the Word of God.

Down the years I have received much help from various communicators and thus the use of this material is not meant to be restricted in any way. I am most appreciative of all the support and encouragement given to me by my wife Joan and the family. To Michael, in particular, I am deeply indebted for all his painstaking work on the wordprocessor - he said he would and he did it! Thanks to Wendy for her efforts in the final stages. I am also most grateful to Geoffrey for his Foreword. To him and to the other friends, who read some or all of the manuscript and made helpful suggestions, I extend my warm thanks. Obviously, the responsibility for the views expressed is mine alone.

Life only begins to make sense and to have genuine purpose when an individual comes personally to know Jesus Christ as Saviour, Lord and Friend. This has been the joyful experience of countless millions worldwide over the millennia and it is my hope that this small volume will be used by God to swell the growing multitude whom no man can ever number.

Introduction

We are literally hurtling through space and it never causes us a moment's thought. In the United Kingdom, scientists tell us that we are rotating at a surface speed of 500 miles per hour (1,000 miles per hour at the equator), as the earth revolves at 66,000 miles per hour around the sun once every year. The seasons come and go as regularly as clockwork and the precision is such that we only take notice if and when any slight variations occur.

The sun, which is our nearest star, is classed as 'average' in size, it is about 93 million miles away and provides for the maintenance of all life on earth. If earth was a little closer to the sun's fiery energy, we would be burnt up, and, on the other hand, if we were a little farther away, we would quickly freeze to death. Certainly we appreciate the vital and delicate balance which guarantees our continued existence.

Earth's satellite, almost one quarter of a million miles away, is the moon which, together with the sun, exerts an immeasurable influence on the earth, especially with regard to the ocean tides. Without the tides and the currents, there would soon be stagnation and death on planet earth. No wonder many believe that our habitation has been specially prepared for us.

And what about the stars? Astronomers inform us that our nearest star(after the sun) is about 4.3 light years distance away. (A light- year actually measures distance and not time and it is equal to the distance that a beam of light travels in one year. It is equivalent to about 12 million round trips to the moon!).

Earth is so remote from the starry heavens that it would take the Voyager spacecraft about 100,000 years to reach Alpha Centauri, our nearest star. It is currently reckoned that there are as many stars as there are grains of sand, that is, 10^{22} or 10 with 22 noughts added - a truly incredible number. And just like each snowflake, each star is different in its properties.

Now we must face the question as to how and why this vastness and yet this detail happened. We have mentioned only a few of the statistics that could be enumerated as we reflect upon the universe in which our solar system is so insignificant. Indeed the solar system is travelling around our galaxy at 500,000 miles per hour, and the contents of the whole universe are in constant motion.

So how did this situation arise? This is a question which has long engaged the mind of man and basically three answers or models are postulated to deal with the question. Not one of us of course was there at the start!

In the first place, it is suggested that what we have today has effectively always been in place. In other words, there never was a start-up date as such. This model has not been widely accepted especially in the West because Science, which seeks to get to the facts, is not happy or convinced by such a notion. Theories based on information gathered to date seem to indicate a start-up time in the past and a likely consummation or change at some stage in the future.

Secondly, there is the evolution model which is favoured by most, but by no means all, of the scientific community. This theory accepts the scenario of a "Big Bang" which is claimed to have occurred at least 15 billion years ago. Our earth, sun and moon were then formed almost 5 billion years ago. Simple life somehow got started at a later stage and this gradually developed or evolved over the vast intervening period until we arrive at today. In this model, early Homo Sapiens people evolved about 150,000 years ago with modern humans arriving on the scene about 40,000 years ago.

To complete the picture, the agricultural revolution got under way around 10,000 years ago. Supporters of this model claim that life on earth took place totally by accident and that, for example, dinosaur DNA is today part of the human DNA. This also means that the birds on the lawn are the modern dinosaurs and also, incredibly, the butterfly and Tyrannosaurus Rex have the same common ancestor.

Lastly, there is the 'special creation' model. This view, based on the Christian bible accepted as the Word of God, states that the Creator God made everything out of nothing in the beginning. Prior to the widespread recognition of evolution theory, belief in divine creation was the norm in religious and scientific circles.

So here we are, several billions of us, rushing through space, rotating and revolving, and at just the correct distance from the sun, our vital star. We enjoy, inter alia, day and night, work and sleep, different seasons, detailed order, personal relationships, etcetera. Basically we have a choice of explanations to consider as to how all developed on planet earth. Was it initial chance or inspired creation? Was it downright fluke or divine fiat? Was it pure accident or the powerful action of God? And these explanations are as opposed to each other as black is to white or as night is to day. There is no place whatsoever for shadowy ambiguity or for sitting on the fence.

In this book we shall examine the evolution and creation models in some detail and also consider the compromise view - theistic evolution - which seeks to harmonise the two models.

Such a study will inevitably lead us to consider Jesus of Nazareth and the position of Israel in relation to the promised Return of Jesus Christ as taught in the scriptures.

We shall also take the opportunity, by way of the appendices, to discuss related topics as wide-ranging as the age of the earth, the Millennium and the key message from 'Atlantis'.

Evolution - Elegant Belief

'Evolution' is a word which, like the word 'charismatic', can mean all things to all men. For our purpose however we wish to regard it in its assumed relationship to the shaping of events on planet earth.

It must of course be appreciated that, even with regard to this particular model, there is a variety of viewpoint and so it is the intention to concentrate on the current Darwinian theory, that is, Neo-Darwinism.

Theories, like fashions, come and go, and at times the most 'rock solid' have had to be seriously adjusted or even abandoned altogether. For example, until recently, it was commonly assumed that the final extinction of the mammoth was to be dated anywhere between 12,000 to 20,000 years ago. Evidence from Siberia now indicates that the proper date was only about 3,000 years ago!

The earlier theory has had to be drastically revised downwards although it is possible of course that some may still cling feverishly to the former notion in order to preserve the vital illusion of tens of thousands of years.

There may sometimes be within us all that feeling of uneasiness with regard to theories - are we being given all the details in order to make a judgment? It is appreciated that there can be the unwitting hoax. For example, it may well transpire, from investigations, that dinosaurs ought to be dated in the more recent past and we shall examine the matter in another chapter.

There has also been an intriguing development with regard to the famous 'Ice Man' found in the Tyrolean Alps a few years ago. He was alleged to be a 5,000-year-old European, actually preserved by a glacier. It now appears that he may not be a European and there is a possibility that he may have been 'planted' there! While the radiocarbon dating is thought to be reasonable, we may have yet another type of hoax and clarification is expected in due course.

Scientists, in particular, should be vigilant and open because 'the man in the street' still has a good measure of respect for them. However if it became known that they were being less than honest with their ideas and theories or of withholding information from the public domain, their ratings would certainly plummet.

Of course we all can make mistakes and these should be rectified as soon as possible after they are discovered. People generally favour honesty rather than cover-up. Situations can be seriously aggravated if, for example, some scientists were to be gagged from putting forward their viewpoint or findings because they were contrary to a more widely held theory. Even less desirable can be cases where employees have difficulty in obtaining posts because their viewpoints do not accord with that of 'the establishment'. Fair play and real appreciation of each other should be the highest aim in all walks of life. We need each other and we certainly can learn from each other. Our minds should hopefully be open to receive information, to judge it carefully and thus to move forward from that point. So often however it is the matter of the 'mind-set' and who among us can fail to plead 'guilty as charged'!

With these introductory remarks, we now turn to review, in the first place, the Darwinian model and secondly to examine some of the drawbacks inherent in the current theory.

Hypothesis

Evolution is linked to the 'Big Bang' scenario which is assumed to have occurred about 15 billion years ago. (We shall examine this view in due course when we consider the age of the earth).

Almost 5 billion years ago, the situation on earth was reckoned to be in order for primitive life, by sheer accident, to have a start. There are competing theories as to how it may have exactly happened and, at this stage, scientists willingly admit that 'Life is Impossible' which was the title of a BBC TV documentary in June 1993. Countless millions of expert research hours have failed to produce the answer for an event which apparently took place entirely by luck. The view is therefore maintained that the conditions were just right at that point so long ago and that a similar situation is not available today. In other words, the start of life was a singularity with no repeatability - it was a real fluke.

And so life got underway, claims the hypothesis, and ultimately we are here today, growing up in the universe. But how, for example, did we humans arrive here? Darwinism rules out the need for a Creator God and seeks to establish a man-made model to explain how it all happened. There are books and articles on the subject which is taught in schools, colleges and universities. The media also promotes the belief at every available opportunity and, from personal experience, there is a marked reluctance to give space to any contrary viewpoint. This is a recipe for a lack of progress.

Today Darwinism stresses the two categories of existence - simple and complicated - and also the two categories of complicated existence, that is, living things (birds, humans) and objects which have been created by living things (paintings, cameras, computers). The complicated things appear to have been designed for a reason and it is impossible that they have come into existence by chance or at random. An aeroplane, for example, has thousands of parts which require to be carefully and intricately put together. While the aeroplane has been designed, the evolutionist postulates that a bird has not been designed. It may be described as a 'designoid' object. The bird looks as if it has been designed but, in fact, it has grown up by an entirely different process which is automatic, unguided and totally unthought out. In a similar manner, the camera lens has been designed whereas the human eye has come together by an equally complex but totally undesigned process which Charles Darwin called Natural Selection. For illustration purposes, the evolutionist might assume that all the component parts of a camera are available and put together so that they were almost in the right order and the camera almost worked. All that is required, he suggests, is a little nudge or random jolt and the almost working camera becomes a working one. All that was required was just a little bit of luck.

This process is then applied, for example, to the formation of an eye by luck. Imagine that we started with an 'almost eye' and so on right back to the very first small piece of luck that got us from no eye at all to almost no eye at all. In other words, instead of making one single gigantic leap, the evolutionist 'smears out the luck' and claims it is an entirely credible sequence of events that gets him from no eye to a perfect eye. This is the Darwinian process of evolution and Natural Selection is his name for the process of 'smearing out the luck'. The claimed essence of evolution is that it takes us from absolutely nothing to something beautiful and complicated without the need for miracles! It is the result of a slow and painstaking process of very tiny steps.

This Darwinian explanation of the formation of an eye has been presented on television on two or three occasions in recent years. It obviously is no more than speculation and the idea that the eye came together in such a fashion caused no small amount of consternation to a good friend, a consultant ophthalmologist, who happened to be viewing one of the programmes.

In general terms, Natural Selection is a hypothesis which seeks to explain the mechanism of evolution. It proposes that the actual variation found in a population leads to greater or lesser chances of survival for different individuals. This in turn affects the extent to which their genes are passed on to the next generation.

The evolutionist claims that each successive change in the process was simple enough, relative to its predecessor, to have arisen by chance. He then asserts that the whole sequence of cumulative steps is anything but a chance process when the complexity of the end product is compared to the original starting point! Cumulative selection, it is said, is the only workable explanation to be proposed for the existence of all the complex designs we see in life.

And the alarming feature is that the Darwinist believes that such a sequence of events actually occurred - at any rate he has the boldness to claim it! It is little wonder that various commentators point out that the evolutionist believes in rather a strange trinity, that is, Mother Nature, Father Time and Lady Luck and, whenever they fail, the ultimate fall-back is 'Abracadabra'!

We must note however that, while the evolution theory is accepted by many scientists and teachers, but by no means all in these categories, it is neither science nor scientific. It is definitely not a fact, and it is properly classed as a belief or postulate which description is accepted by evolutionist authors. Evolution has not been witnessed by human observers, it cannot be tested experimentally, and, as a theory, it is so skilfully constructed it is not capable of falsification. It is so plastic or pliable that it has the ability to explain anything and it is widely used in such a manner as we have noted.

The belief is certainly elegant and it leaves similar

ideas very much in the shade. If there is really no Creator, then Darwinism must be top of the list as a theory. Once things got underway in the dim and distant past, there was that steady, staged development. There was no miraculous leap at any juncture, just a slow gradual process which appears to carry with it the inevitability of progress and achievement. Today this is how the model stands and, while it is claimed to be well able to cope with the various situations, its advocates no doubt reserve the right to amend or improve it as the need may demand. There is literature on the topic including books by Dr. Richard Dawkins, the Oxford University zoologist, who also gave the Royal Institution TV lectures over Christmas in 1991.

Hurdles

A Creator!

Adherents of Darwinistic belief openly admit that it is impossible to prove there is no Creator and this will invariably be the case no matter whatever further advance there is in knowledge. There is such wonder and vastness about us that it would be foolhardy to write off the possibility of the Almighty. In effect, there is an admission by the evolutionist that his theory starts with only 50% chance of being successful. This point was immediately conceded by Dr. Peter Atkins who, on TV, in the 1993 Oxford Debate about God, promoted the opinion that evolution accounted for everything there is today.

The Darwinist therefore enters the contest or debate

with one hand tied forever behind his back. He will readily point out that the believer in a Supreme Being is similarly placed because his belief may also prove to be wrong. There is however an unbridgeable gap in the two positions. If the believer is ultimately mistaken in his viewpoint, he loses nothing while if the evolutionist or atheist is wrong he loses everything in the eternal context - a frightening prospect.

This of course raises the key question as to why anyone should wish to go through life with obvious uncertainty in respect of a potential afterlife, which has been and is believed by the vast majority of mankind. As always in such matters, there is a strong clue in the Christian bible which we shall examine in due course. Suffice to say at this stage, that the bible indicates that it is the foolish person who claims there is no God (Psalm 14:1). This does not mean that God does not exist, but only that the individual has made a conscious decision to live his life without reference or accountability to God. He may appreciate the wonder and beauty of the world but he has convinced himself that this all started by freak accident. In effect, he deliberately takes the glory from the Creator and bestows it on the creature. The bottom line is thus one of resistance, indeed open rebellion against such a God and to persist in this attitude is to court eternal ruin. God's verdict on this outlook is that those who profess themselves to be wise in these matters have actually become fools in his sight (Romans 1:21-23).

Complexity at the Start!

Darwinists theorise that the start of life in the primeval soup or whatever 4.6 billion years ago had to be something very basic, that is, a single cell. After all, it happened by a fluke as somehow life developed from non-life. This,in itself, is a concept which scientists find very difficult to accommodate and life has still not been achieved after much experimentation.

In fact, the simplest cell has been and is far too complex to have arisen spontaneously. Everything had to be right from the start and it was impossible that the first life form diversified, adding new genetic information to its DNA by chance mutations. Mutations are generally neutral or harmful, and not beneficial. There is no known mechanism to account for this unending development from an assumed simple position to one of endless variety and complexity today. The evolutionist is however duty bound to believe that this gradual unguided process did actually take place because he has no need for God in his belief.

At heart, the Darwinist is very much the modern 'fundamentalist'. He adopts a particular view, not based on genuine observed evidence as we shall see, insists that his approach is the only correct one and openly attacks anyone who is willing to advocate another method. His position is untenable because he has deliberately locked himself into one model which even he confesses may be incorrect. He is willing to adopt a basically hopeless position simply because he has decided not to even consider the other view.

The Fossil Record

Charles Darwin firmly believed that, in due process of time, the fossil record would have yielded legions of transitional and major-change fossils in accordance with his theory. This has not proved to be the case and it puts another large query against the whole evolution hypothesis. Indeed, had Darwin been alive today, he would most likely have had to admit that what he always feared had materialised, that is, there was no intermediate fossil evidence and therefore his theory should be immediately abandoned. The fossil record clearly implies that the 'missing links' are still missing even after more than one hundred years of careful search. In the 'showcase' of evolution, the special places reserved for the in-between specimens are still unfilled and unlikely ever to be filled. The fossil record shows the consistent pattern of sudden appearance followed by stasis, that is, a lack of change and this is contrary to the Darwinist hypothesis.

The evolutionist of course has to seek to respond to such an unwelcome situation and his theory is pliable enough to permit him to make such an attempt. He admits that there is by no means the fossil evidence, but it appears to him that there may possibly be a few examples (some top-level scientists would however refute such a claim). What is more likely is that future excavations in the right places would produce the missing items. It is even possible, he postulates, that there was an evolutionary spurt, thus nullifying the necessity for any intermediates. While the evolutionist accepts that slow gradual development is the norm, there is also some scope for the quick spurt in small groups - what is termed the 'Punctuated Equilibria' theory.

At the end of the day, the Neo-Darwinist should seek to gain support for his view from the fossil record. This would clinch his case and the most recent link in the chain is clearly the best place to search, that is, from apes ultimately to humans. If such a link can be established beyond all reasonable doubt, it would certainly go a considerable distance to giving approval to the supposed earlier evolutionary stages. However it must be kept in mind that John Eddy, the well known American astronomer, admitted about fifteen years ago that, with some frantic recalculation, he and others could live with Archbishop Ussher's timescale of 6,000 years for the age of the earth and sun !

This was a remarkable statement which indicated that the vast aeons were unnecessary from his viewpoint. With the removal of such a timescale, there was of course the implicit confirmation that Darwinism was dead without any hope of resuscitation.

Marvin Lubenow has researched the fossil information in respect of so-called 'ape men' and humans, as provided by evolutionists themselves, and he has clearly shown in his book *Bones of Contention* that humans were contemporary with or even earlier than the 'ape men' and therefore humans could not be evolved from them. This is the same sort of picture all the way back in the fossil record. There is no conclusive evidence to support the evolution hypothesis because, if there was, the matter would have been agreed and disposed of many years ago. It was David Pilbeam of Yale University - an expert in the study of human ancestors - who confessed that: 'If you brought in a smart scientist from another discipline and showed him the meagre evidence we've got, he'd surely say, "forget it; there isn't enough to go on"!' This incredible statement appeared in Richard Leakey's book, *The Making of Mankind*, on page 43. Leakey, in stating that he and others cannot take this advice, admitted 'we remain fully aware of the dangers of drawing conclusions from evidence which is so incomplete'.

Dating Difficulties

It should be stressed, at this juncture, that when similar results are presented claiming to come from independent sources, this is not always the case. Each scientist or research worker does not have the time, the opportunity or the ability to check out what his colleagues are doing in their own disciplines. On the basis of integrity, information or dating or whatever is accepted but often it is not appreciated that the details emanate from a particular mind-set. For example, it is common practice to ignore results or dates which are wildly at variance with an expected answer, to insert a footnote where there is not a large margin of difference and to clearly publish what is the most persuasive in the main text. A top scientist once confessed that generally the theory came first and this influenced the evidence sought while the public would reckon it happened the other way around.

Once again, there is an abundance of literature on

this interesting topic of dating by means of, for example, the radioactive carbon 14, uranium-lead and potassium-argon methods.

Richard Milton deals with these and related matters in his book *The Facts of Life* and shows that of the many methods of geochronometry - measuring the earth's age - all are subject to uncertainties. However the Darwinist adopts a particular method of dating as this appears to yield an age for the earth of billions of years. Some other methods, which do not depend on radioactive decay, indicate an earth that is much younger and it is these which have been neglected. We shall look more closely at this topic when we come to consider the earth's age.

In brief, in dealing with the radioactive decay method, it is necessary to know the position at the start of measurement, whether the rate of decay is constant over the long period and also what, if any, were the outside factors. For example, if there was a worldwide flood some thousands of years ago, then this would have had an immense impact on decay rates. When such factors are taken into account, and it is impossible to measure them, it means that dating is not as straightforward and reliable as was initially thought.

Most geologists take the uniformitarian view that 'the present is the key to the past'. They assume that as nothing dramatic is happening today to the earth, this has always been the case in past history. For dating purposes, this means a very slow and regular build-up of sedimentary rocks (that is, fossil-bearing rocks) and, on this basis, the earth must be billions of years old. But such a simplistic view ignores floods, ice age, droughts and meteor strikes in earlier times and the impact of such events is incalculable. Someone has well said that, to put events into real context, 'the past is the key to the present'!

Some readers may possibly have forgotten about the eruption in May 1980 of Mount St.Helens in Washington State, USA. An earthquake caused massive rock slides with devastating consequences. In all, it was estimated that the output of energy was equivalent to 20,000 Hiroshima-size atom bombs. Six hundred feet of stratified sediments were built up in a matter of a few hours. Any geologist, not knowing exactly what had occurred, would assume that the strata had been normally deposited over a period of hundreds or even thousands of years. And this was only one small local event, in comparative terms. The impact of other major catastrophes would be incalculable and this type of situation is now having a considerable bearing on the geologist's current viewpoint. 'Catastrophism' is once more firmly on the agenda.

The Darwinist knew he needed lots and lots of time for the outworking of his gradual evolutionary process. It was essential for his theory to have the remotest chance of acceptance. The geologist with his Geological Column,seemingly spanning long periods, was able to provide the time. As a result, a sort of academic relationship sprang up and developed between the two sciences. If an evolutionist was having problems with dating a particular fossil, he turned to the geologist for assistance. Similarly, if a geologist wished help to date a rock stratum, he requested an evolutionist's opinion on the fossils it contained. In this type of link-up, rocks could be of help to date fossils and fossils to date rocks. It is undeniable that the claimed millions of years and the fossil record go hand-in-hand and are inseparable. And no account is properly taken as to how fast the rocks were initially formed in the Geological Column.

The results of experimental research, presented by Guy Berthault to the Fourth French Congress of Sedimentology at Lille in late 1993, showed that strata build up rapidly in a sideways motion and not simply one upon another. This means that a fossil in a lower rock stratum may actually have been buried later than one in a higher stratum! Clearly this has a major impact on the position of a stratum in the Geological Column which can say nothing about the relative time when the rock was laid down. Once again, the vital time basis for evolution theory is effectively challenged.

Other Issues

There are other matters putting the embattled evolution theory under the severest pressure. Top international scientists representing disciplines such as genetics, chemistry, palaeontology and sedimentology have recently combined to speak out against the hypothesis by means of a video presentation. A university professor, who gave the 1992 Royal Institution TV Lectures, also publicly urged his colleagues not to ignore observed evidence in favour of preconceived ideas. Various authors and commentators from inside and outside science have heavily criticised evolution dogma and especially the attitude of Darwinian fundamentalists.

It is common knowledge that there is a quest for a more credible explanation as to how evolution proceeds. Darwinism is simply unable to cope with all the recent observed data with which it has been bombarded. Almost every week, scientific items on the radio, TV and press tell of new findings which indicate more and more the incredible wonder and complexity of all that is around us. Scientists are being asked to accept that all this information, which can only come from an intelligent source, started by a freak accident and then somehow developed over endless millions of years. Such a diet has proved too much so that increasing numbers of scientists worldwide have set aside the evolution belief because, in reality, it totally fails to answer the questions.

At least one or two key issues need to be addressed. It is only appropriate that this disquiet about Darwinism is better known in the public domain. The impact of such perverse teaching in schools, colleges and elsewhere also requires examination and revision as a matter of urgency. Over the next few years, textbooks hopefully will be altered although even today some theories previously discarded by evolutionists still appear. There unfortunately exists a form of scientific censorship and no matter how inadequate the current paradigm it will only be replaced if and when a more acceptable model is produced.

Special studies are proceeding with regard to the human brain which of course is extremely complex. Currently it is not thought to be well represented as a powerful logical computer. Its development is rather like a form of natural or neural selection and this concept is based on extensive research with young babies in the USA. In reaching, for example, for a particular item or toy, the baby will initially make numerous mistakes but, in due course, will soon be able to grasp the object at possibly the first attempt. The selection process is thus, to a large extent, being strengthened and inbuilt.

The importance of such a situation dare not be forgotten in the spiritual realm. Youngsters will naturally tend to espouse or select those ideas or beliefs with which they are reared or brought into contact at an early stage. It is therefore vital for young people to be introduced to the things that pertain to God, from as early an age as possible. It is only the entrance of God's Word which gives true light.

Some will be unfamiliar with the Gaia Hypothesis promoted some years ago by Dr. James Lovelock. (Gaia is the Greek goddess of the earth). Basically, the earth is to be regarded as a 'living planet' in that life is thought to be an all-or-nothing affair which either takes over a planet completely or does not achieve any grip or hold at all. Earth is therefore considered to be a living planet rather than merely an abode of life.

One aspect of the Hypothesis however commands our attention. Most of us are now aware that the amount of carbon dioxide in the air is rapidly increasing because of our activities. It is estimated that the concentration of carbon dioxide has increased by about one quarter in the last one hundred years. If this continues, the planet will warm as the greenhouse effect gets stronger.

Some people regard Gaia as a sort of Mother Earth figure who will look after us all and ensure that somehow natural processes will remove the carbon dioxide which we are steadily pouring into the air. On the other hand, Lovelock has suggested that Gaia may wish to look after herself and, in so doing, may remove us from the scene ! The Hypothesis is suggesting that we are now approaching the end of a long period of stability (in evolutionary terms) and perhaps Gaia may be heading for a convulsion in which the temperature will rise dramatically before some new mechanism hopefully evolves to again stabilise things. There is therefore the thought of unbearable conditions. It is perhaps more than coincidence that the bible points to a coming day of judgment when the earth will be burnt up and this subject we will consider in a later chapter.

Concluding Thoughts

Darwinian evolution is no more than a weak human attempt at an explanation for the origin and development of life on earth. This hypothesis which is neither fact nor science, proceeds without the existence of a Creator. Its adherents however frankly confess that it is impossible to prove there is no God in control and this admission is one of many objections to the theory.

Increasing numbers of scientists worldwide have been casting off the yoke of evolution dogma while it is an open secret that a more plausible explanation of the theory is urgently required.

The Darwinian hypothesis is currently the best on offer to those who deliberately dethrone the Creator and also ignore the dearth of genuine evidence.

Evolution requires two essential ingredients. Firstly, a very long timescale in order to accumulate all the intermediates and, secondly, a mechanism guiding each step in some particular direction. The idea that gradual cumulative natural selection is the explanation for our existence calls for a supernatural level of faith.

Perhaps astute readers have spotted the inherent contradiction in the Darwinian hypothesis. In one place, Natural Selection was said to be 'automatic and unguided' and yet, in another, it is claimed to be a 'mechanism guiding each step in some particular direction'. Now the interesting feature is that both these contrary descriptions are directly linked with one of the most prominent Darwinists in the United Kingdom!

If assumed selection is unguided, miracles are necessary to account for today's situation. On the other hand, if there is vital guidance in the process, it is more than obvious the Source from whom such direction emanates.

There are at least four main objections to Neo-Darwinism among various sections of the scientific community. Firstly, the so-called history of life on earth has not been one of slow continuous process. There have been periods of standing still, evidenced from the fossil record and also living plants. Secondly, mutations are not beneficial and cannot produce entirely new forms of life. In the third place, there is the obvious sheer improbability of the whole idea. A theory which effectively requires an endless succession of mathematical miracles cannot be right, is the view of many mathematicians and not a few biologists. Finally there is simply not enough time for the 'molecules to man' scenario to take place. It is not that an extra 4 or 14 billion years would be adequate to allow for so-called simple life to arise and become complex by natural processes. Such time frames are far too brief by countless orders of magnitude. And of course additional aeons would be a hindrance rather than a help because there is clearly much more scope for inevitable harmful diversity. (It is also a fact that since the scientific age no new animal species has been observed to emerge).

Some years ago Sir Fred Hoyle and Professor Wickramasinghe claimed that, in their view, Darwin had been thrown out. Professor Jack Ambrose, the cell biologist of London University, also stated that, in his opinion, the creative view of the origin of life no longer needed to be defended against the evolutionary argument as it was actually the evolutionist who was in retreat.

The 1993 Royal Institution lectures on TV were given by Professor Frank Close. He carefully peeled back, as it were, the 'cosmic onion' to move from the atom to the nucleus and then to the proton and neutron particles. But even this was not the end. Each of these minute particles is comprised of three other entities, in certain fractions, known as quarks and for all we know there may still be much more detail to be discovered. As Professor Close concluded that part of his lecture, whether scripted or involuntarily, he suggested that God is a mathematician ! Such a remark is reminiscent of Einstein's famous comment : 'God does not play dice'.

As usual, there are two ways of looking at all of the recent discoveries. We may totally applaud man, who supposedly arrived on the scene by accident, or we may bow in wonder and submission before the omniscient and omnipotent God who is light and who dwells in unapproachable light. Jesus declared: 'I am the light of the world. Whoever follows me will never walk in darkness, but will have the light of life' (John 8:12).

The Bible - God's Revelation

In any discussion of the past, present and future, it is impossible to avoid consideration of the background, teaching and worldwide influence of the Word of God, generally known as 'The Bible'. It contains, inter alia, a vital message from God and this is often referred to as 'The Gospel', which means 'Good News'. Many read and study the bible, quote from the bible, swear on oath on the bible and, when people wish to underline their integrity on a particular matter, they may well adopt the expression: 'It is the gospel truth'. Why should this be the case and why should the bible always be the world's best seller?

The bible is unique in the world of literature. In reality, it is a collection of sixty six books inspired by God and penned by many authors, spanning a period of thousands of years. Its basic setting is in the Middle East and the bible purports to cover the period from the start to the finish of 'time', as we know it. It is therefore much more than man's attempt at a 'Grand Unified Theory' - it clearly sets out 'God's Unalterable Timetable'.

The bible claims to be the Word of God the Creator and Sustainer of everything there is. God is disclosed in the Old Testament, that is, before the incarnation of Jesus Christ, the Son of God, and also in the New Testament. The Old Testament scriptures are chiefly, but not entirely, related to the Jewish nation but in the New, with the first coming of Jesus, there is a world-wide inclusiveness which is in sharp contrast to the Old Testament exclusiveness of Israel.

At this stage, some Jews still anticipate the coming of the Messiah based on their understanding of the Old Testament scriptures. Christianity, however, as against Judaism, accepts both the Old and the New Testament scriptures and declares that God's Messiah has already come in the person and work of Jesus. Jesus is now in heaven and he will return in the future to administer final judgment. This is generally referred to as the Return of Christ, or Second Advent, which will be studied later.

Christians stress that the truths of Christianity are 'revealed' by God, that is, they are by no means the consequences of human endeavour or discovery. Thus the scriptures are regarded as authoritative, permanent and sufficient and they have final authority over all personal judgments. To seek to have a proper understanding and interpretation we must honestly submit ourselves to the authority of the Word of God and to the direction and enlightenment of the Holy Spirit, the Third Person of the Triune God. Christians generally accept that, where the scriptures appear to be plain, specific and uncompromising, there is an onus on them to adopt a similar stance. Where however they seem not to be specific on any particular matter it would be unwise to be dogmatic.

'But why should the bible and its teaching be given the topmost priority?' is a question to which an answer must be sought.

Christianity is by far the most widespread of all religious faiths and, as it is based on Old Testament Judaism, it is therefore among the oldest in the world. In general terms, Christianity has the allegiance of a vast number of the world's population and this figure is swelling on a daily basis. As we shall consider later, the claims made 2,000 years ago by its founder, Jesus of Nazareth, were and are unique and unparalleled in the history of the world.

It is therefore the height of folly to fail to come to grips with such a universal movement. From a mere handful of people in a weak and insignificant Roman province in the middle East, Israel, this faith has steadily spread since then and is currently growing worldwide at a faster rate than ever before.

Christianity, which specifically teaches a special creation by God, cannot be ignored. This assumes an even greater importance when, as we have already seen, the adherents of evolution frankly admit that their model cannot be guaranteed. After all, it is only a theory. It is utterly impossible to conclude there is no God.

The bible naturally takes the Creator for granted, that is, as a fact and there is never any attempt in the scriptures to prove that there is a God. Indeed the bible is not so much concerned about creation as it is about 're-creation', that is, the redemption of mankind, the forgiveness of sins and similar vital matters.

In summary, God's Word details the following historical events:-

(i) In the beginning God purposed and created the

heavens and the earth and pronounced everything 'very good' (Genesis 1:31).

(ii) He gave every advantage to our 'first parents', who were made in the image of God, with only one prohibition to test their obedience (2:17).

(iii) Eve, deceived by the serpent, and Adam listened to the tempter and they sinned against God in disobedience (3:1-7). As a consequence of the Fall, mankind inherited the sinful nature which is ever rebellious against the Creator.

(iv) Sin and wickedness increased on the earth in the ensuing thousands of years to such a marked degree that God had to judge the inhabitants with a catastrophic flood, saving in the ark only Noah and his family and representatives of the animal kingdom (Genesis 6).

Many have pondered who exactly were the 'Sons of God', referred to in Genesis 6:2,4. These were not fully identified and different suggestions have been advanced over the years. They were of the godly line of Seth (and not of Cain). Perhaps they were supernatural creatures, other than angels who do not marry. Perhaps they were men who were associated with a special priestly ministry to whom such a title was given. There is obvious depth and mystery in this particular portion and so it would be unwise to be dogmatic.

(v) Through Noah and his family (four couples), God re-peopled the earth and also enlarged their diet (Genesis 9:3). He commanded the inhabitants to spread out but, in disobedience, they decided to stay together to build a city and tower (of Babel) in order to make a name for themselves. However the Lord upset their machinations, confused their one language so that they spread out worldwide as he had initially commanded (11:1-9).

(vi) The earth was divided or separated in the time of Peleg (10:25). We shall consider this occurrence in due course.

(vii) God, ever mindful that he wanted people to live in harmony with himself, later chose Abram in Ur of the Chaldees, that is, modern Iraq, and made him the father of the Jewish nation (Genesis 12). Jacob (or Israel) was the name of Abraham's younger grandson while his twin was called Esau, the father of the Edomites.

(viii) About 2,000 years after the time of Abraham, Jesus was born in Bethlehem in the land of Israel. He was of the human line of Abraham and the renowned King David but was also declared to be the Son of God (Romans 1:4), the Son of the Most High (Luke 1:32). Because he was and is the God-Man (the Divine-human), he was able by his substitutionary death on the cross of Calvary to reconcile mankind to God. The Almighty indicated his total satisfaction in that Jesus was raised from the dead. Indeed it was utterly impossible that the grave could retain the One who is the Lord of Life (Acts 2:24) and Jesus now reigns on David's throne (Acts 2:30).

God had dealt with the age-old claims of sin and had also established a just basis for forgiveness extended to all who confessed their sin and placed their faith, their trust, in the living Lord Jesus Christ.

(ix) Since the death and resurrection of Jesus who returned to the glory of heaven, the Holy Spirit of God, through the ministry of the church of Jesus, is engaged in convincing people of their sin and their need to trust in Jesus as personal Saviour and Lord. This ministry will continue unabated until God commands the consummation followed by the Judgment and the ushering in of the eternal state. 'Time', as we now know it, will be gone and gone for ever.

So then, why give close attention to this message of the bible? Basically because it has the real ring of truth about it and deals with us in our own experience. The scriptures do not flatter us but tell the story of our inner being in all its ugliness, 'warts and all'. We could never do that of ourselves because we naturally tend to be blind to our own faults and biased in our own favour. But God knows all about us (John 2:24,25).

Mankind generally seeks to reach out to the Unknown and this is specially evidenced when new tribes are discovered. Such invariably have some form of worship, for example, the spirits of ancestors, the trees or the heavenly bodies. However the bible teaches that it is the Creator who comes seeking those whom he has made. Without the revelation of the bible, man has no genuine idea who he is, what he is doing or where he is going. His answers to these searching questions are no more than hunches and provide no sure foundation for daily life.

God declares that he created man, that is, male and female, in his own image. This is of course a spiritual resemblance rather than a physical appearance. We shall look more closely at this aspect later but at this stage we simply note that humankind is of male and female, and that there is the inbuilt need to worship or believe in someone or something.

The outline description is simple and straightforward and yet majestically comprehensive. There is no way in which humanity has had to wait until now to really understand God's revealed message and his omnipotence.

The book of the beginnings, that is, Genesis, clearly teaches that God is a God of immeasurable power and order and this is confirmed in what we see around us and within us. In the West especially, this has resulted in very large strides being made in such fields as research and applied science. During past years many scientists simply stated they were 'thinking God's thoughts after Him'. It often goes unnoticed that rabbits give birth to rabbits and humans to humans and so on. If this was not the case now and in the past, the situation does not bear even a moment's consideration!

The early chapters of Genesis tell of actual lands and nations which we may still identify today. The sheer ring of authenticity in chapter 2 is staggering. A man was created on his own by the Almighty before a woman was made from his body. This information is vital to the record and stresses the eye-witness nature of the narrative.

Genesis tells of sin and disobedience against God. It tells of dastardly murder, brother of brother. There are details of agriculture, city building and the making of artefacts and musical instruments. The record tells of some seeking God and walking with him while the vast majority ignored their Creator and went their own way. We have not the slightest difficulty in relating to any of these situations and we feel certain that we are part and parcel of them, a sort of 'deja vu'. Little wonder one bible writer, King Solomon, declared that there is 'nothing new under the sun'. The old Chinese proverb however makes the telling point that 'the only thing people learn from history is that people learn nothing from history'!

Genesis tells of an original environment of God's goodness but which was later devastated in the catastrophic judgment of the Flood. It should also be noted that Noah's ark, until the middle of the nineteenth century, was the largest sea-going structure ever to be made. Not only was its capacity remarkable because of its three decks, but marine experts tell us today that the special measurements made the ark virtually unsinkable. And to make matters more illuminating, this structure, which took many years of expert workmanship to build, was made when the concept of rain was unknown. This type of situation is experienced today, for example, in parts of Namibia where there is no rain only a mist, a dampness received from the nearby ocean.

Population growth experts also confirm that the world's current population can be derived from Noah and his family. By God's providence and grace, they survived the Flood which may be dated at least 6,000 years ago. It is important to state that any dates are no more than approximations because, outside the bible, there is little recorded history against which to fully authenticate them.

Perhaps now is the time to refer to the longevity of the people who lived before the Flood. Their life spans were given in terms of many hundreds of years which was not the position post-Flood. All sorts of schemes have been suggested to reduce their ages to levels consistent with current experience. There is of course no need to embark on such excursions. What God purposed and created was initially ‘very good’ and it was only the results of sin which caused the marked deterioration.

We need to remember that Moses was linked with the writing of the Pentateuch, that is, the first five books of the bible, and it was he who used the different life spans without having the need to provide explanation. He had no difficulty in stating that Adam died when he was 930 years old, Abraham died when he was 175 years old and yet he was able to describe the events related to the year-long Flood. Indeed there is no other portion in the Old Testament where the happenings of one single year are detailed to such a remarkable degree and this was at a time when people lived for hundreds of years.

The book of Job is regarded as one of the oldest books in the Old Testament. Bible commentators confirm that it is set in the Middle East and is perhaps to be dated around the time of the patriarch Abraham. There are various references to snow and ice and their impact. These were unknown prior to the Flood which totally changed environmental conditions to those which we experience today.

Everybody sits up and takes notice when someone prophesies an event or events and later they occur. If it happens once, there is the possibility of pure coincidence but, when it re-occurs, we realise the truth. Let us now reflect on some such situations in the bible.

When Adam and Eve disobeyed God, he judged them but also promised that the seed of the woman would crush the serpent's head and that the serpent would strike his heel (Genesis 3:15). In the first place, the unusual expression 'the seed of the woman' and not of the man is to be noted. Jesus was born of the Holy Spirit (Luke 1:35) and he crushed Satan, the serpent, by his life, death and resurrection. He purchased our salvation at the cost of his precious blood. Secondly, we note that the time between the giving and the fulfilment of the promise may have been 10,000 years at least!

About 4,000 years ago, God promised Abraham that, through his seed, the Son of God would be born and also his natural descendants would be a vast number. These commitments were fulfilled to the letter. Even the very birthplace of Jesus was prescribed hundreds of years earlier. Added to these were the prophecies that the nation of Israel would reject their Messiah and would suffer accordingly. These are now events of history with special reference to the most severe judgment upon the nation at AD70 which we shall consider later. It must also be noted that the Lord Jesus himself foretold the coming desolation at AD70 during his own ministry (Luke 21:20-24).

In Acts 17:26 we read a very specific statement

made by the apostle Paul to the effect that God made every nation of men from one man and this is of course a reference to Genesis 1:27. Scientists now agree that there is only human race although they did not always accept it. The remarkable fact is that Paul, 2,000 years ago, was not giving a prophecy for today but was actually relying on the trustworthiness of the Word of God which had stood the test for thousands of years of earlier history.

It must be recognised that all of us, scientists included, have only finite knowledge. 'The best of men are only men at their best'. Just because there is not an answer to a particular problem today does not mean that there is not an answer. Over and over again the bible has been shown to be accurate in so many areas and none more especially than in archaeology. It was not long ago that the so-called experts claimed that the bible was wrong with regard to the Hittites. However they continued with their digging and established the existence of these people.

It is only being honest when, within ourselves, we acknowledge a sense of love and justice and so on. We are distressed when people fight with and kill each other and, in local situations, we want justice done and to be seen to be done. Attitudes such as these do not naturally arise from within but are God-given. We are so much more than a large collection of molecules - we are spiritual and immortal! It is also most interesting to note that more than 90% of secular songs relate to the relationship between the sexes. This is the way God set it up in the beginning and we wonder what would have transpired if men and women hated instead of loving each other!

The Almighty knows the end from the beginning and he is to be fully trusted. In any areas of uncertainty, our reliance should be on God and the scriptures rather than the obvious fickleness of man.

Finally, we notice some of the indicators to immortality. In the first place, there is the reality of the unseen. Things are not always what they seem to be and we are almost certain to be wrong if we simply judge by outward appearances. We have travelled a great distance from the standpoint which identifies the real with the concrete. It is precisely the things which we cannot see that are the most basic in the universe. Love, truth, personality and conscience, for example, are also invisible and yet it is obvious that such unseen spiritual forces are the bedrock reality out of which the whole complex structure of life and history is hewn.

Secondly, there is the rationality of the universe. As an experiment, assume the abandonment of belief in the hereafter. We now must believe that life has produced this marvellous thing called personality with its vast array of powers only to destroy it in the end. We have to accept that the universe, having toiled over a long period to produce its crowning glory, proceeds to dump it on the scrap-heap of death. We also have to believe that people who have brightly shone with hope and faith and honour can be irrevocably silenced by a virus, a bullet or an accident.

Such is the position to which we are logically forced by the denial of the scriptural teaching with regard to immortality. It is the unbeliever who has to reduce every trace of purpose about us to myth and moonshine. Clearly the Christian faith is difficult and demanding, but what of the alternative ? It is by its outlook of eternal hope that Christianity makes real sense of the universe. Rejection of such a vista brings problems more intractable than those from which many try to escape. Indeed the alternative to the position as set out in the Word of God involves a surrender of intellect which many see as an outrage to demand.

Other signposts to immortality include the character of God, the vital personal experience of regeneration by the Holy Spirit and, of course, the reality of the resurrection of Jesus Christ (John 3:16 and 17:24. Numbers 23:19. Ephesians 1:13-14. 1 John 4:13. Acts 1:1-3. 1 Corinthians 15:3-8). These aspects are generally covered throughout the book.

Creation - Divine Handiwork

The bible precisely and clearly states that the Almighty created and controls all that there is. (We shall consider the matter of dating in a later chapter).

This truth is above and beyond our greatest imagination. Due to our finiteness, we have consciously or unconsciously reduced the Infinite One to the tiny scale of our activity and understanding. This means that the Word of God should always be first and foremost in our thinking and in our living.

The Triune God, in his sovereignty, specially ordered all the arrangements so that the universe is what we have today. If the components were different to even a small degree, the universe would also be different.

The Almighty, who is incalculable (Job 26:14) set up the universe (Genesis 1), he sustains and uniquely controls it (Hebrews 1:3) and, in the fulness of time, he is going to dissolve it to establish a new heaven and a new earth (2 Peter 3).

Today we are understanding more and more of the scale of the universe and in so doing, in a very small measure, we are appreciating God's omnipotence. The heavens and the earth reveal his glorious handiwork (Psalm 19) and also his special care for mankind (Psalm 8). In return, our hearts and lives are to be offered to the Lord of All in worship and service.

Genesis chapters 1 and 2, John 1:1-10, Romans 1:20-25, Colossians 1:15-17 and many other portions of the bible declare that God made everything. The writer to the Hebrews (11:3) teaches that we understand, by faith, that what is seen was not made out of what was visible. In other words, the Creator made everything out of nothing and without this revelation, mankind is totally in the dark. Our own little theories or ideas are no more than fallible guesswork.

The Almighty spoke and it was accomplished (Psalm 33:6-9). He declared everything to be 'very good' (Genesis 1:31). Moses had first-hand experience of the awesome power of God. He witnessed the divine activity in the deliverance of Israel from Egypt and also the miraculous provision for such a multitude in the forty years of desert wanderings.

Days

Genesis 1:5 contains the words: 'and there was evening and there was morning - the first day'. This type of expression was adopted on another five occasions in the chapter. It is essential that we understand what Moses is seeking to convey. The regular use of 'evening' and 'morning' indicated well known defined times. Such words were to be found throughout the Pentateuch and they referred to actual historical situations. It is therefore incredible to imagine that Moses was giving a special meaning to the expressions in Genesis chapter 1 without making this exception crystal clear. Indeed, to couch God's revelation in a simple straightforward manner and then to expect his readers to understand something totally different is to be grossly unfair to Moses who had been very well educated and trained in his early years at Pharaoh's court.

We are dealing with historical records in Genesis. God's ordination of work for six days and rest on the seventh or Sabbath was also recorded in the book of Exodus 20:11.31:15.35:2, in Deuteronomy 5:12-15 and in other scriptures. Many commentators on the Hebrew are clear that Moses was referring to typical days and not long periods in Genesis 1. This was the message he wished to stress. Today we find it difficult to accept because we know more about the vastness of the universe than Moses did. The obvious temptation is therefore to play down the scriptures in order to make them more palatable for others and ourselves. Our failure is to realise that God is omnipotent and therefore absolutely nothing is impossible to Him. To see the Almighty as being restricted in any way whatsoever is to have a total misconception of the God of the bible. On one occasion, the Son of God spoke to those who questioned him about the resurrection. He said: 'You are in error because you do not know the scriptures or the power of God. God is not the God of the dead but of the living'. (Matthew 22:29-33). This was a stern rebuke to the Sadducees as it is to us if we tend in any way to be like-minded. As we rely entirely on the Lord for our life, our hope and indeed our everything, this also ought to be our position with regard to his revealed creation. It is vital that our trust is ever in the Word of God and not in the ways of sinful men. It was Augustine who said: 'Believe in order that you may understand.'

'Understanding is the reward for faith.'

Once we set aside the obvious meaning of the word 'days' as a short-period, consecutive measurement of time, we cannot explain it and therefore various ideas and suggestions are set loose. We shall comment on some of these later in the book.

Food

We find it easy to fail to identify the nature of the food which God provided for his new creation. Genesis 1:29,30 states that it was every seed-bearing plant and tree. This was remarkable in at least two respects. In the first place, it meant that the Creator prohibited the eating of flesh although this restriction was lifted after the Noachic flood (Genesis 9:3) when conditions became totally different on earth. God's handiwork in creation was perfect in every respect so that there was ample provision for the small as well as the large creatures. Lush vegetation and even giantism were the order of the day and this has been often confirmed by those who work in these earth sciences.

Secondly, there was no special reason for this particular food supply of plants and fruit to be mentioned. Indeed, if it had not been detailed, this lack of information would have perhaps caused no concern. The fact however that it was recorded indicates its antiquity because Moses would have had no personal knowledge of this early prohibition. He lived thousands of years after the events in Genesis 1 so that the information was actually handed down to him or else the Lord revealed it to him. Either way, it is a remarkable piece of knowledge throwing light on yet another aspect at the dawn of creation.

People

It is interesting to note that the names of Adam and Eve, who were made in the image of God, were never mentioned by Jesus in the Gospels although the apostle Paul referred to the actual names in some of his letters. There was no doubt whatsoever that Jesus had our 'first parents' in mind when he pertinently remarked that God made them 'male and female at the beginning' (Matthew 19:4). He was somewhat surprised that his questioners, the Pharisees, either had not read or had forgotten the details contained in Genesis chapters 1 and 2. God made them, brought them together and placed them in Eden where there was a garden (Genesis 2:8). The rivers which were mentioned in the chapter help to locate the area in the Middle East where God set them and this would provide an indication about the colour of their skin -they were not 'white Europeans'! Once again the sheer antiquity of the record is evident. The Creator made Adam initially on his own. Genesis 1, in filling in the overall picture, did not make this point which was highlighted in Chapter 2. The female was taken by God from the male, from his side and not his head or foot! Eve was described as the mother of all living and this statement needs to be underlined because some, without authority, have tended to ignore the fact in their treatment of the early chapters of Genesis.

We should carefully note that the word 'man'

(Genesis 1:27) includes both male and female. Biblically, male and female need each other to be complete. The message today for the church and the community is one of complementarity, of harmony and definitely not a matter of the male seeking to lord it over the female. There was and is of course the divine order in that Adam was created first before Eve and the man is therefore designated as head (1 Corinthians 11:3). Paul however tenderly stressed the goal in Christian marriage when he wrote that the wife should reverence her husband who should, in turn, love his wife. And the greatest love of all was and is Christ's love for his church (Ephesians 5:22-33).

Before leaving Adam and Eve, the bible makes it abundantly clear that they were able to communicate with God and with each other (Genesis chapters 2 and 3). This was the position from the outset. Indeed Adam named all the living creatures (2:20) and any interpretation which ignores this is to be firmly rejected. Once again the evolutionist is left with still another of his many 'mysteries'. He has to concoct some sort of scheme in which apes become ape-men and later become men who stumble on a way to communicate.

The Darwinist knows that men can communicate in the fullest sense and, as he will not admit that there is a Creator, he has to revert to his own brand of evolutionary magic which may possibly convince him but nobody else. It is vital to record that apes or chimpanzees have never talked or ever will talk. This is because they lack the speech centre in the brain and the special throat and mouth muscles necessary to form words.

There is no evidence that human language evolved from animal noises and studies indicate that the oldest languages are much more complicated than modern ones.

Heavenly Bodies

God made the 'greater' and 'lesser' lights and also the stars to mark seasons, days and years and to give light on the earth (Genesis 1:14-18). Jesus made a most interesting comment when he said that God provided not 'a sun' or 'the sun' but actually 'his sun' for everyone's benefit (Matthew 5:45). Indeed without 'his sun', life is impossible and it goes beyond the bounds of belief for anyone to honestly claim that this arrangement just simply happened!

In early days, people worshipped whatever they felt to be appropriate. It might be someone or something above them or around them or actually of their own manufacture. For many it might have been the heavenly bodies so Moses stated that God made them thus showing his majesty and superior power. Where the Almighty was and is not known or revealed, nations are without guidance and are therefore wayward.

While the sun, about whose processes we cannot today be absolutely certain, and the moon are relatively close to the earth, stars which are balls of seething gases are large distances from us. There are countless billions of stars and each was given its own degree of splendour (1 Corinthinans 15:41). They certainly brighten up the night sky and some of the bible writers developed the theme of the people of God shining in service and witness (Daniel 12:3. Philippians 2:15). The scriptures indicated that the stars gave light on the earth from the 'fourth day'.

The 'Big Bang' scenario for the first moment of the universe is now very popular with many, if not all, scientists and we shall review the concept when discussing the age of the earth. On backward extrapolation, which on any basis is most suspect and unreliable, the heavenly bodies formed almost five billion years ago. Bearing in mind the fallacies which evolutionists have developed in dealing with the evidence all around them on earth, it behoves us to be ultra careful with regard to their speculations about deep space where no one has ever been. We admit that there is so much that we, as finite creatures, will never understand. It is however instructive to note that, in Big Bang cosmology, the assumed original tiny fireball of mass and energy exploded in the first 300,000 years of the life of the universe, to give structures more than 500 million light years across the universe. Space itself therefore expanded at a rate of almost 1,700 times the speed of light! The Old Testament declares that God 'stretched out the heavens' and no doubt there are other dimensions about which we know nothing.

While the Big Bang model proportionately links distance and time, these aspects are unrelated in the biblical revelation. The writer to the Hebrews states that 'the universe was formed at God's command' (11:3). To mix a Big Bang timescale with God's record of creation is plainly absurd.

Some have been unduly concerned about the existence of light before the sun was created. Firstly, we note that the bible states that God initially created light without a secondary source and we know today that all that is needed to have a day-night cycle is a rotating earth with light coming from one direction. It is also interesting to recall that, in the eternal state, there will actually be no need for sun or moon (Revelation 21:23). In the second place, having light before sun, actually underlines divine inspiration. A human author would surely have modified the record to suit his own understanding. Having 'day' without the sun would naturally have been inconceivable to the ancients.

Living Creatures

At the word of the omnipotent God, the waters teemed with living creatures, the birds flew above the earth and the land produced all kinds of animals (Genesis 1:20-25). All these creatures were made perfectly from the outset, otherwise they would never have functioned at all. The fossil record bears witness to the accuracy and completeness of God's unerring handiwork. Evolution has no place in the bible and it is only a concept in the minds of the doubtful or rebellious. The sheer wonder of the world about us is breathtaking and even those who do not believe in God are willing to admit it. Evidence abounds to conclusively show that the evolution of living animals, including many high profile examples, is no more than a bankrupt theory, as we have noted in an earlier chapter. The caterpillar which changes into a chrysalis and then emerges as a butterfly, the insects which undergo one or two drastic changes during their life cycle, the most unusual bombardier beetle, the crafty sea slug and the co-operation of the hermit crab and the sea anemone all defy the Darwinian hypothesis.

Review to Date

We live in a vast universe and this demands a fair-minded explanation. Our little world is just right for us. There is a truly remarkable variety in the skies, on the earth and in the seas. Above all other creatures, we have the brain capacity to seek to understand ourselves and all that is around us. We look at our hands, our feet, our eyes and at our skin which is thankfully the way it is-what a prospect if our skin had happened to evolve to be transparent! The more we get to know, the more we realise how little we actually do know. We are still, as it were, on the shore looking out to the vast oceans of knowledge and adventure and regularly there are new discoveries of what was already available but which had remained hidden for a long time.

Because we are the way we are, we instinctively ask the crucial questions: 'How did all this happen and how is it likely to end?' Our quest is for satisfactory answers.

The Darwinist theorises that life on earth started by a sheer accident. He promotes his model, admits there are many holes in it but is ever hopeful that his elusive and conclusive evidence will turn up some time in the future. His theory is elegant and has a measure of acceptance but, at the end of the day, it is nonetheless only a hypothesis. To the open mind, knowing that we cannot go back to the start, it seems incredible that it all worked out so well. We feel certain that we are not going to evolve into some other creature as apparently is suggested in past ages. If this is the best model currently available, some people will stick with it until a better or more convincing one arrives on the scene. At the back of our minds however there is an uneasy feeling because it all seems to be too good to be true - just like a fairy tale - and we are also acutely aware that thousands of scientists, as a result of their own investigations, reject the belief. Many people claim that evolution, which is today an anti-God system, is no more than man-made speculation based on prior speculations and it is therefore valueless.

The whole idea of evolution is really not much more than wishful thinking. 'The likelihood of the chance formation of even the simplest protein from inanimate matter is a one with 40,000 zeros after it. These figures are big enough to bury the whole theory of evolution forever', as Sir Fred Hoyle put it. T N Tahmisian, Director of the US Atomic Energy Commission, stated that scientists, who teach that evolution is a scientific fact, are no more than con-men as 'the story they are telling is the greatest hoax ever'.

But there is another viewpoint which is much more in keeping with the observed evidence. This model, detailed records of which go back literally thousands of years, states unambiguously that God made everything we see in accordance with his own will and purpose. We admit the wonder and intelligence that is all around us. We see creatures in their complexity and realise there was no genuine mechanism by which they could have developed and survived on a gradual, piecemeal basis. There is within everyone the strong desire to worship and when we personally come to know this God through his Son, Jesus of Nazareth, who lived our life and died our death, we know we need search no further. Ours is that abundant life and peace which we long for others to receive and enjoy. We hear again the joyful message of the Christmas angels that, in Bethlehem, the Saviour of the world has been born - born for us! And there can only be peace on earth when all the glory is given to God in the highest!

Theistic Evolution - Unprofitable Compromise

As its name suggests, the theistic evolution model claims that the Almighty used or guided evolutionary processes in order to produce all the wonder and diversity we enjoy today. God started it all off and, as required, stepped in to ensure that everything gradually evolved to completion.

God is thus depicted as choosing to operate by means of evolution and, to be realistic, this theory is not much more than a compromise. It acknowledges the Creator God of the bible and, at the same time, the belief is able to accommodate evolutionary dogma.

The Darwinist boldly asserts that God is irrelevant as far as his model is concerned but he is no doubt pleased to note some Christians leaning in his direction to an extent. On the other hand, Christians who accept a comparatively recent creation, which rules out evolution, complain that a distinct advantage has been accorded to the Darwinist in that the Word of God has been diluted in their view. At the end of the day, the theistic evolutionist has been able to please no-one but himself, if he has even achieved that!

We have already discussed the hurdles associated with evolution and wish to record that if the Darwinist had actually to prove his theory he would be unable to do so. His is a belief and it will never be anything other than a belief. And the hurdles and problems applying to basic evolution also apply to the theistic evolution viewpoint.

Theistic evolution naturally comes into real tension with the biblical revelation which conveys that the Almighty, in creation, used action and not lengthy processes. God spoke or acted and it was so (Genesis 1 and 2. Exodus 20.11. Psalm 33,95,104,147 and 148) and it is eminently fair to state that, on a plain reading, the scriptures know nothing about theistic or any sort of evolution.

The theistic evolutionist has been convinced that the earth is very old, that is, almost 5 billion years old, and this is one of his key reasons for promoting the theory. In so doing, he had hoped to somehow reconcile the creationist and the evolutionist but this aim was never achieved. In effect, the proposed solution caused more problems than it actually solved and it has been firmly rejected by scientists and writers of both the creationist and evolutionist camps.

It is customary for theistic evolutionists to make assumptions for which there is no scriptural support. For example, while admitting that Adam and Eve are the first human beings in the bible, they will seek to insist on the probability of non-human hominids living before our first parents! The plain straightforward meaning of the bible is thus challenged in order to give some substance to their theory. If the earth is billions of years old, the theistic evolutionist has to deal with the fossil record, which is not a record of life but, in fact, a record of death. Evolution teaches that the process occurred via death, and it is hardly a method that God would adopt to create a 'very good' world (Genesis 1:31)!

The bible declares that death and violence only came into the world as a result of Adam and Eve's rebellion against God. Were not all the animals originally vegetarians as commanded by God in Genesis 1:30 ? If there was no death or bloodshed before the sin of our 'first parents', then how could they have, as it were, 'dead' animals (fossils) in the ground beneath their feet in the Garden of Eden? The Lord Jesus came to die because of what occurred in a literal garden when a literal Adam and Eve rebelled against God.

The apostle Paul, who wrote under the Spirit's guidance 2,000 years ago, stated that Adam and Eve were the first humans of God's creation - the head of Eve was Adam and the head of Adam was Christ (1 Corinthians 11:3). There is nowhere in scripture the slightest allusion to other types of creatures on earth before our first parents and such must only be introduced because of a belief that the earth is old. Evolution, which is foreign to the bible, is needed to support the requirements of a man-made notion of an ancient earth which is very suspect as we shall later discuss.

Theistic evolutionists will sometimes draw attention to the illustration of the overthrow in judgment of the towns of Sodom and Gomorrah to seek to justify that the Noachic flood was also local. This however misses the whole point of the Lord's reference (Luke 17:26-30). Totality and suddenness are the vital ingredients of the message with the venues being of minor importance. The 'days of Noah' were by no means localised and the Lord and Peter referred to Noah's flood as a solemn picture of universal judgment at the

Second Advent. Peter even used the word 'kosmos' relative to the situation. From the descriptive vocabulary in respect of the event and its duration (Genesis 6-8), Moses was depicting a scenario of worldwide devastation. As wickedness was widespread, so also was the resultant judgment. If the Flood was literally no more than a local happening, it is a recorded fact that such events have often occurred during the subsequent course of human history. In effect, this means that the Almighty has been unable to keep his covenant promise as set out in Genesis 9.

In conclusion, theistic evolution theory is an unprofitable attempt at harmonising two irreconcilable models. The evolutionist has no place for God and so he has no time for the theory. In order to promote it, the theistic evolutionist is however compelled to dilute or interpret the scriptures in such a manner as to attempt to show that the Almighty adopted evolutionary processes in creation. Such an approach, which generates far more problems than it solves, is unacceptable to the vast majority of Christians.

Adherents of theistic evolution have, at best, an inadequate understanding of the awesome power of the Almighty. At the other extreme, they generally set aside most of the early chapters of Genesis as historical narrative. Once the realities of direct creation, rebellion, the Fall and the universal Flood judgment are so treated, the door is inevitably opened for the remainder of the bible message to be similarly mishandled. Thankfully, however, theistic evolutionists rarely follow the logical consequences of their downgrading of Genesis.

Jesus of Nazareth

The Place

A visit to Israel, or the Holy Land as it is often referred to, is not to be turned down if the opportunity arises. In this small country (length about 240 miles and breadth around 40 miles) it is impossible not to marvel at the changes in the land. There are stretches of sandy shores on the Mediterranean coast, lush and rich valleys and mountainsides, rambling foothills and flat plains, skybound peaks, body-parching hot wilderness climbing from the mineral-saturated waters of the Dead Sea, the lowest spot on earth. Whatever Israel is, it cannot be said to be uniform! There is variety all the way from snow-capped Mount Hermon in the north of the country to barren desert in the south.

Hermon is generally thought to be the Mount of Transfiguration in the Gospels (Matthew 17:1,2) although some hold the view that Mount Tabor, in the vicinity of Nazareth, was where Jesus was transfigured before his 'inner three' disciples, Peter, James and John.

In the deep south of the country, since reverted to Egypt, lies the monastery of Saint Catherine, dating from around the 4th Century AD. Here the world famous 'Codex Sinaiticus' was uncovered last century by the scholar Tischendorf. This oldest complete bible is also to be dated about the 4th Century and, after many eventful travels, it was purchased by and now resides in the British Museum.

Israel is steeped in history and the bible certainly comes alive for those who are fortunate enough to be able to visit the country. While Jerusalem, Bethlehem, Jericho, Qumran (of the Dead Sea Scrolls' fame) and Masada are in all of the tourist itineraries, it may happen that Nazareth, in the northern half of the country, is bypassed. To the west of the sea of Galilee, Nazareth is set on a hill (Luke 4:29) and today has a population of around 80,000 with Arabs comprising about 50,000 and a Jewish development of 30,000.

There has always been a genuine spirit of co-operation in this busy bustling town and this is especially marked in the hospital service. One such hospital is affectionately called 'The Hospital on the Hill'. It is often referred to as the 'English' hospital but it is actually owned and run by the Edinburgh Medical Missionary Society (EMMS). This interdenominational Mission was founded in 1841 and the commencement of a small Christian medical clinic in Nazareth dates from 1861. EMMS has the distinction of being the oldest Medical Mission in Europe and arguably the oldest in the world. In the operating theatre on any day, there may be two Arabs, one a Christian and the other a Muslim, a Jew and a Christian expatriate, all seeking to co-operate in service. The hospital exists to glorify God, to share in reconciliation and to bear witness to God's love so clearly manifested in the life and ministry of Jesus of Nazareth.

The Person

King Herod, almost 2,000 years ago, asked the vital question: 'Who is this Jesus?' (Luke 9:9) and it is still being asked today in a worldwide context. To seek to answer such a question there is only one source document - the scriptures of the Old and New Testaments.

Right away we need to recall that Nazareth is not mentioned as such in the Old Testament while the title 'Jesus of Nazareth' is to be found in the four gospels and in the Acts of the Apostles. That the Messiah was to be born in Bethlehem was the subject of Old Testament prophecy (Matthew 2:3-6) and yet Matthew (2:23) stated that Jesus was to be called a Nazarene, that is, someone from the Nazareth area.

This is something of an enigma but perhaps there are one or two clues to assist us. When the apostle Philip told Nathaneal (or Bartholomew as he may be called) that Jesus was the long-awaited Messiah (or Christ, the Anointed One), Nathaneal replied with the guileless words: 'Can anything good come out of Nazareth?' (John 1:45,46). Nazareth, set in 'Galilee of the Gentiles', was ranked of little importance by the average Jew. It was basically 'off the beaten track', the sort of place one could readily be pardoned for giving 'a miss'; indeed Nazareth was regarded by many as being no more than a backwater. And it is the Messiah's meek and lowly aspect which is sometimes stressed in the prophecies, for example, Isaiah 53. In this sense, Jesus was described as a Nazarene.

This is how the Almighty works. He comes to us in the Incarnation, not with royal fanfare so that Jesus is born, not in splendour, but uniquely 'wrapped in strips of cloth and lying in a manger' (Luke 2:12). His birth which effectively changed history and dating from BC (before Christ) to AD (in the year of our Lord) was unheralded and unrecognised except for the few whose spiritual eyes had been opened by God as they waited in hope for the fulfilment of the Old Testament promises (Luke 2:25-38).

The apostle Paul rehearsed a similar theme when he reminded the church members at Corinth that God has his own method of doing things which may be in direct contrast to the ways of the world (1 Corinthians 1:18-31). And so it is with God's creation. The glory and the wonder are all around us if only we have the eyes to see. We see but do not appreciate, we hear but do not understand and thus we resemble the Jewish nation who refused to accept their Messiah (John 1:10,11). However the picture is quite different today as increasing numbers of Jews openly confess Jesus as their Messiah and Lord.

The bible makes it abundantly clear that Jesus is none other than God the Son. He is uniquely the God-Man and people from all walks of life down the ages have found this to be true in their own lives and experiences.

In the scriptures we see the essential deity and the perfect humanity of Jesus. He is the one who grows up in favour with God and men in the relative obscurity of Nazareth (Luke 2:51). He is called the carpenter and his mother, brothers and sisters are well known in the local community. And yet Jesus declares that, in reality, whoever does God's will is his brother and sister and mother (Mark 3:31-35)!

What is God's will? Jesus spells it out in one of his many discussions with the Jews - to believe that he is the one sent by God is the will and work of God (John 6 : 28). Jesus is the one and only way to God the Father, indeed to see Jesus is to see God (John 14:6-10).

A careful reading of the gospels indicates that Jesus and his church, which he is building, are unique. His claims and actions are both clear and extraordinary. C.S.Lewis, the converted atheist, wrote that Jesus was either mad or he was who he claimed to be although some sceptics would suggest that Jesus was simply mistaken.

Around Easter time in 1992, I attended a debate in Edinburgh between Dr. Richard Dawkins, the Oxford zoologist and atheist, and the Archbishop of York, Rev. Dr. John Habgood. During the subsequent question time, Dr. Dawkins indicated that, in his opinion, Jesus was simply a Jewish teacher of his time, that he was mistaken about various matters and never claimed to be God or the Son of God.

Such a notion however is at variance with the source document. The Jewish authorities were totally aware of Jesus' blasphemous claims, as they regarded them, and hence they plotted and carried through with his crucifixion. Death however could not hold Jesus and he arose victoriously, having completed the work his Father gave him to do. On the cross, the Saviour did not cry: 'I am finished'. His cry was one of conquest, of victory: 'It is finished'.

An honest study of Matthew 11:20-30, for example, will dispel any doubts that Jesus was somehow mistaken about his identity and mission. This chilling message is crystal clear and yet in it there is real encouragement for all to come to Jesus for rest.

The Proclamation

Jesus, preceded by John the Baptist who was the only son of his mother's relative Elizabeth, and who was also the Elijah of the New Testament, came proclaiming the gospel message: 'The time has come, The Kingdom of God is near. Repent and believe the good news!' (Mark 1:15).

John pointed to Jesus as the one who was more powerful, more worthy than he and who would baptise with the Holy Spirit (Mark 1:8). In the first chapter of the apostle John's gospel, the Baptist also identified Jesus as God's Lamb who was to take away the sin of the world (1:29). The animal sacrifices of the old economy covered sin but, in complete contrast, Jesus dealt with sin by completely removing it. Jesus, because of his substitutionary death at Calvary, atoned for sin which separated mankind from the holy God so that our sin has been tossed into the sea of God's forgetfulness never to be dredged up again. What a relief for believers that, as far as the east is from the west which today we appreciate in its widest scope, so far has he removed our sin from us (Psalm 103:11,12). And as we share the bread and the wine, we remember and give thanks for Jesus who gave himself for our salvation.

Each new movement has its clarion call, its watchword and, for Jesus, this was 'The Kingdom of God'. (The full title was 'The Kingdom of the God of Heaven' but this was usually abbreviated to 'The Kingdom of God' or 'The Kingdom of Heaven' or simply 'The Kingdom'). The Kingdom loomed large in Jewish thought with its basis and expectation in, for example, the Old Testament book of Daniel (2:44,45 and 7:13,14). In New Testament times, the Jewish nation was under the heel of the Caesar from whom they longed for release. There was therefore utter contempt for those who collaborated with the Roman oppressor. Tax collectors, for example, became rich by overtaxing their own countrymen thereby lining their pockets. Zacchaeus of Jericho was one such person but when he really believed in and received Jesus, he became a visibly changed man, a true spiritual son of Abraham (Luke 19:1-10).

The nation, on the basis of their interpretation of scripture, looked forward to the day when they would be no longer in subjection but would again be in the ascendancy. They wistfully remembered the golden age of the past - the times of King David and King Solomon - and they longed for a restoration. Even the disciples had this idea very much in mind as Jesus left them to return to glory; 'Lord, are you at this time going to restore the Kingdom to Israel' (Acts 1:6)? Had Jesus not taught them to pray to their Father in heaven: 'Your Kingdom come, your will be done on earth as it is in heaven'? (It is informative to note that while Islam lists the so-called 'ninety nine beautiful names of God', the name 'Father' is not one of them).

The Jews, with their aspirations set on the material 'here and now' objectives, had failed to appreciate who their enemy really was. It was not Rome but was actually Satan and sin. Jesus came exclusively to deal with such an enemy. Rome could never keep an individual from trusting in God but sin, unconfessed and unforgiven, could separate a person from God for all eternity. The gravity of sin is measured by the fact that it took the Son of God to the cross to purchase our salvation. God forsook his Son so that he could freely welcome us to himself, into his Kingdom. It cost God his all to provide us with the unspeakable gift of eternal life in his own dear Son. No wonder the writer to the Hebrews declares that there is no escape for those who reject God's salvation (Hebrews 2:1-4).

Jesus came proclaiming the Kingdom at just the right time. Surely it was the carol writer who got the timing incorrect when he penned that the offspring of the virgin's womb came 'late in time'! Paul was to state in Galatians 4:4 that Jesus came in the fulness of time, that is, he came in accord with God's timetable. Man will seek in vain his own 'Grand Unified Theory' while, from eternity to eternity, there is 'God's Unalterable Timetable' for those who have the eyes to perceive it.

The first coming of Jesus was at the right time politically, morally and strategically and the messengers travelled along the Roman roads with the life-changing gospel of Jesus of Nazareth, the One who died and rose again. With the solid benefit of the Roman peace, the first Christians reached out with the joyful message of inner peace with God. They shook the world - they turned it the right way up! There was the severest of opposition and persecution, as Jesus had foretold. 'To be faithful to death' did not mean until one died but to be faithful even though it meant death.

'Jesus is Lord'. The living Lord had saved them, thrilled them and possessed them with his matchless undying love. They willingly gave their lives to him who had laid down his life for them. (No one, for even a moment, would remotely consider laying down their life for the cause of an evolution belief even if it was couched in the grandest of terms!).

Within a few centuries, the Roman emperor Constantine had publicly confessed Christ and all was changed. The visible church has had its ups and downs, but ultimate victory is inevitable. In Daniel 2 we read that the stone cut without hands, that is, divine and not human, grew from a very small beginning until it filled the whole earth.

Jesus said emphatically that he would build his church and that absolutely nothing could stand against its forward march. He would brush aside the gates of hell's citadel (Matthew 16:17-19) and that is what he is manifestly doing throughout the world.

The 'strong man', Satan, has been bound by a stronger than he and it is Jesus the Almighty who plunders the spoil to lead countless souls to glory. He is the author, the leader, the trailblazer. It is he who endured the cross, despised its shame and sat down at the right hand of the throne of God (Hebrews 12:2). Jesus is worthy of all honour and praise and glory and to such themes we shall give attention when we consider the glorious Second Advent. 'The kingdom of the world has become the kingdom of our Lord' (Revelation 11:15).

In the ministry of Jesus, there were myriad references to the Kingdom. He invested much in the concept and of course drew so much from it with the result that many books have been and will be written on the subject. The Rev. Professor J.S.Stewart, in his excellent book entitled, 'The Life and Teaching of Jesus Christ', described the Kingdom in specific terms. Looking at it on a personal basis, the Kingdom is moral not nationalistic, it is spiritual not material and it is actual not ideal. Bearing in mind that it was in essence a Kingdom, a community that Jesus was passionately concerned about, Professor Stewart also shows that the Kingdom is social and not individualistic, it is universal and not local, and it awaits a final consummation because it is coming and is not yet complete.

The Kingdom is basically something which is inward and personal and can only be entered by the 'new birth' (John 3:3). It is supranational and links together all whose hearts, minds and lives are freely surrendered in allegiance to the risen Christ. As Jesus did not come to be served but to serve, so he desires his friends to do likewise. Such an attitude will not happen automatically but will gradually occur as our wills are daily yielded to the Spirit of God. Love, joy, peace, patience, etcetera, is actually the fruit of the Spirit and not the fruit of the saint! (Galatians 5:22-24). As it was remarked on one occasion: 'It is not difficult to be a servant until someone treats you like one!'

God's Kingdom may only be entered by anyone who receives it as a little child (Mark 10:13-16). The rich young ruler wished to achieve it, to earn it, as it were, like a reward. But it does not happen in this way. Like a child we are to divest ourselves of our importance, our money or whatever so that, with open empty hands, we may receive the gift above all gifts.

One Sabbath, early in his ministry, Jesus spoke in the synagogue of his home town of Nazareth. He quoted from the book of the prophet Isaiah (61:1,2) and proclaimed that the prophecy was fulfilled in him and in his ministry. This declaration stands for all time and is a challenge to any who would wish to see Jesus in some other light. When he however developed the teaching that God's loving care stretched out to everyone beyond the limited boundary of Judaism, the congregation was incensed and attempted unsuccessfully to hurl him over a nearby cliff.

Today the gospel is being made known to the ends of the earth and more and more people receive the Word of God in their own languages. Individuals, families, communities and even nations are being changed by the grace of God. There is satanic opposition, to be sure, but still the Kingdom is extended. Many people desire to know God personally because they have been created in that fashion. They desperately need the scriptures which alone can provide real light and bright hope.

In the bible we read of Jesus going about doing good and yet, by cruel hands, he was crucified. But God was not defeated in his purposes. The Almighty raised him from the dead and now offers forgiveness of sins through his one and only Son, Jesus of Nazareth.

'Nothing in my hand I bring
Simply to thy cross I cling
Naked, come to you for dress
Helpless, look to you for grace'.

Reliance upon nation, creed, profession or good works or intentions is of no saving value. It is only the way of the cross that leads home-in both the Old and the New Testament.

Conclusion

In God's perfect timing, the promised Messiah was born 2,000 years ago in Bethlehem and subsequently grew up in Nazareth, a town in 'Galilee of the Gentiles'. Jesus came to heal and to call for repentance as he preached the good news of the Kingdom. He came not to be served but to generously minister to others and finally to die on the cross for the sins of the world. The Lord Jesus rose victoriously from the grave (first the Cross and then the Crown) and his life-changing message of forgiveness of sins and hope was proclaimed by the church. Today this selfsame gospel is being made known to earth's remotest bounds.

'I stand amazed in the presence
of Jesus the Nazarene
And wonder how he could love me
A sinner, condemned, unclean'.

The Return of Christ

A Controversial Subject

If there is one subject above another about which Christians in general will disagree, it is the Return of Christ or the Second Advent. The basis of the disagreement is not the Return of the Lord Jesus but the events and timetable both before and after this momentous event. It is accepted that after the Great White Throne judgment (Revelation 20) the final eternal state will be ushered in by God. In other words, God's creation in a past age will run its course until the end of time whether this occurs in the reasonably near future or in a rather distant period.

As the Kingdom was limited to Jewish hands, starting with Abraham, for about 2,000 years, it is thought by some that the Kingdom may be of longer duration in Christian hands because of the very much wider sphere of responsibility and service.

From another viewpoint, events have recently tended to move more quickly than at any time in the past and therefore the Return of Christ may perhaps be nearer than anticipated some years ago. All are agreed however that 'the times and dates' are unknown (Acts 1:7) although some commentators suggest that certain events may indicate the approach of the Second Advent.

There is abundant literature available on this key topic so that all the main views may be studied by the interested reader. It is however fair to stress that the majority tends to read the books which support their own approach and fails to grapple with the material supplied by another school of prophecy. While I have had the opportunity over the years to consider all the main Advent views, which may be a good or a bad thing, it is the intention not to go into too much detail. We shall look first of all at what I believe to be a sound biblical approach. Later we shall consider Israel and its future and then briefly review aspects of the major prophetical schools. It is appreciated that some readers may be better informed than others. However as the subject is very much a part of God's programme in scripture, it is only right and proper that we accord to it the care and attention it thoroughly deserves.

What Saith the Scriptures ?

The Bereans (Acts 17:11,12) were commended in that they were willing to search the scriptures to confirm the teaching they received from Paul. Indeed the Lord Jesus directed that we should study the scriptures because they spoke of him (John 5:39,40). One important aspect of the Holy Spirit's gracious ministry is to lead us into the truth about Jesus so that we may know him more and more. Our aim should be to compare scripture with scripture as far as possible and to follow the three 'golden rules'. In the first place, any book must be looked at in its setting. Secondly, a text must be seen in its context, because, if removed, it may readily become a pretext. Finally, it is only proper to move from the straightforward to the more difficult areas and not the other way around. For example, it would be totally unjustified to take a firm view on a verse or verses in the book of The Revelation, which is admittedly very difficult, and seek to impose that view on another clear portion of scripture so that it is distorted or, worse still, is rendered meaningless. Another important matter is to consider how the inspired New Testament writers deal with the Old Testament scriptures. 'In the Old the New is concealed; In the New the Old is revealed'. In other words, when required, the weight or balance should be accorded to the New Testament approach and not vice versa.

The Certainty of His Coming

It is only the exceptional Christian who does not firmly believe in the Second Advent of the Lord Jesus Christ. The New Testament is especially clear on this matter and the apostle Paul identified the Old Testament 'Day of the Lord' with the Second Advent (1 Thessalonians chapters 4 and 5). In the letter to the Hebrews, the writer stressed that Christ was sacrificed once to take away the sins of many people and that he will appear a second time, not to bear sins, but to bring salvation to those who wait for him (10:28).

The Return has been promised by the Lord Jesus in the Gospels (John 14:3), prophesied by the angels at the Ascension (Acts 1:11) and preached often by the apostles in the Acts and the epistles (Acts 10:42. Titus 2:13. 1 Peter 1:3-5). Almighty God will announce 'Time Out' and will proceed to wrap up everything and usher in the eternal state, that is, the New Heavens and the New Earth as the former will pass away (Revelation

21:1). It is important to note that, when Paul wrote to encourage and comfort the believers (1 Thessalonians 4:13-18), he stated that the Lord will come with a loud command, the archangel's voice and the trumpet call of God so that no-one will be in any doubt about the event.

The Uncertainty of the Timing

The Second Advent is compared to 'like a thief' on one or two occasions(2 Peter 3:10). This is the hallmark of uncertainty because a thief will never send an advance warning! Although we do not know 'the times or seasons', 'day or hour', there have always been those who thought they knew better.

Even the first disciples largely misinterpreted the teaching about the Kingdom of God. After the resurrection, they still had in mind the establishment of an earthly kingdom in the comparatively near future (Acts 1:6). However Abraham, the father of the faithful, and the others had rightly set their hearts on a city and on a better country - the heavenly objectives (Hebrews 11:8-16).

A careful reading of Paul's letters to the Thessalonians indicates that some had actually stopped working because they wrongly expected the Lord's imminent Return.

In and around the year 1000 AD many anticipated the Second Advent and no doubt the same will apply at the end of this millennium. The Lord Jesus indicated, in one of the parables, that 'after a long time' he would return (Matthew 25:19).

Over the past one hundred and fifty years, many

preachers had worked out their schemes and dates as part of their teaching. They were certainly wrong and as such only served to bring the scriptures and the Return into disrepute. Words such as 'imminent', 'soon' and 'in this generation' were used and are still being adopted today in some circles.

Many will be unaware of the Irvingites who claimed that 1864 was to be the time. The Millerites also calculated a date of 22 October 1843 and when nothing happened they rechecked their sums and stated that they were one year out - the date became 22 October 1844 and we know the result!

Charles Scofield, of the Scofield Bible, went into print to claim that, based on his calculations, the Advent was very near in 1914. And it ought to be remembered that the sect of Jehovah's Witnesses previously claimed that Jesus did actually return in 1914 and then went into hiding!

Earlier this century, well known bible scholars on the subject of prophecy often taught the soon Return of the Lord but again and again they were shown to be wrong. And of course, when the European Union expanded to more than ten members, this meant that other notions, based on the ten toes of the image in Daniel 2, had to be quietly abandoned.

The scriptures give a stark warning about false prophets. If what they say or promise does not actually come to fruition they are to be so judged. We must all be open and admit that we mortals do not know the time of the Second Advent. As there was no date given for the First Advent so there is no date for the Second. All will take place in the fulness of time in accordance with the Almighty's timetable.

Our Service While Waiting

How then are we to live as Christians? There is a real need for us to appreciate that whether or not the Lord returns in our lifetime, in a few years, we will die and leave this scene of time so that, effectively, for us the Second Advent is just around the corner. The Word of God encourages us not to be slothful but to be positive in our service for the Master. We are to seek to occupy each day to the glory of God. It should be our constant aim to live holy lives, to encourage and support each other and to reach out in practical concern to those who do not know the Lord in that personal and vital way. Indeed there is an abundance of helpful instruction in 1 Thessalonians chapters 4 and 5 to enable us to live God-glorifying lives. At every stage of our Christian pilgrimage, there is always to be that necessary interaction between God and ourselves (2 Thessalonians 2:13-3:5). The essential relationship of the child of God to his heavenly Father cannot be overemphasised. Daily prayer which is God-directed, believing and persistent has achieved and will achieve what is, humanly speaking, impossible. Nothing is beyond the reach of prayer except that which lies outside the will of God.

God, by his Spirit, now indwells his children. We are to be filled by the Spirit and to be led by the Spirit. If we decide to go our own way on occasions, we quench the Spirit as light and grieve him as love. The Spirit's ministry has been likened to the wind (John

3:6-8). Ours is not to seek to puzzle about the wind's mystery. Ours is, in faith, to hoist the sail and to be blown and directed by him in all of life's journey. Ofttimes we can be like half-filled vessels attempting to overflow! The real secret in the Christian's service is not how much we have of the Spirit but how much he has of us!

The Resurrection and the Judgment

'Man is destined to die once and after that to face judgment' (Hebrews 9:27). Clearly God's Word knows nothing about the notion of reincarnation!

Jesus often spoke of the resurrection, the judgment and separation. Indeed he made many references to heaven and hell and indicated precisely that any who did not believe in or commit themselves to him will not be with him in heaven (John 8:21). In Matthew 7:24, Jesus described the wise man as the one who both hears and obeys his words while in chapter 13, in the parables of the weeds and the net, he pointed to the inevitable harvest and judgment at the end of the age.

As far as the Lord was concerned, the present and the future plainly divided into two categories, that is, this age and the age to come (Matthew 12:32). At the end of the present age, there will be the resurrection and the judgment which none can avoid (Matthew 11:36,37 and John 5:28-30). The basis of judgment will not be the strength of our protestations, 'Lord,Lord', but our personal relationship to and service for our Lord and Master (Matthew 25).

Jesus stressed that we do not know the time of the

Advent and therefore each one needs to be ready to give account (Matthew 24:42-51). Interestingly, he stated that while two may be sleeping, another two may actually be working (Luke 17:34,35) and some have taken this to be an indirect reference to our rotating earth.

The fact, importance and teaching about the Old Testament judgment at the time of the Noachic flood must never be overlooked. The Lord referred to its occurrence and dire consequences and thereby he confirmed future judgment (Matthew 24:36-41). Inside the ark there was strong security for Noah and his family, while outside there was universal ruin.

There is a certain coming judgment by fire (2 Peter 3). An ark as such would be totally inappropriate not only because of the nature of the judgment but also because, at that time, there will be countless millions of believers on the earth. However God will change them 'in a flash' (1 Corinthians 15:51-53) and remove them from the fiery bath as indicated in 1 and 2 Thessalonians. At the same time, the Almighty will change all who have died in Christ in past ages thus further underlining the exceeding greatness of his power which he displayed at creation. The apostle Peter made reference to God's protection of Noah at the time of the Flood and also pointed to the appropriate security God will provide when the heavens will be destroyed by fire and the very elements will melt in the heat (2 Peter 3:10). It should also be recalled that the Lord and Peter regarded the Noachic flood as worldwide as Moses obviously meant it to be so understood in Genesis 7.

Future judgment is indisputably universal as was that in the Old Testament dispensation. Two of the indications of the 'last days' are the rejection of the Second Coming and the deliberate forgetfulness that the Flood actually destroyed the world of that time.

The apostle Paul, led by the Spirit of God, adopts the same approach to the resurrection and to judgment as his Lord and his fellow apostle. Indeed the Nicene Creed takes up Paul's message in 2 Timothy 4:1 that Jesus will come from heaven 'to judge the quick and the dead'. This doctrine is repeated in Paul's other epistles. Previous references have been made to 1 and 2 Thessalonians and these extra scriptures should also be noted (Acts 17:31 and 23:6-8. Romans 2:15,16. 2 Corinthians 5:10,11).

In the penultimate book of the bible, Jude, 'the servant of Jesus Christ and a brother of James' also reminded his readers of the unavoidable judgment of God which will occur on the Great Day.

The Almighty is ever active in time. Scriptures indicate, for example, his judgment on the antediluvian world, the Egyptians at the time of the Exodus, the Canaanite nations, the Israelites themselves, the Babylonians and others. However the Word of God plainly teaches that there will be the 'Great Assize' at the end of time (Revelation 20 and Matthew 25). All will be summoned and not one will be missing. The record books, including the book of life, will be opened and unerring judgment will be dispensed. The King will judge righteously and every mouth will be stopped. His verdict will be eternal joy or 'the second death'. It is wisdom of the highest order to now make our peace with the Judge of all rather than face the consequences of a chilling 'guilty' verdict. 'It is a fearful thing to fall into the hands of the living God' (Hebrews 10:30,31).

In conclusion, the Word of God plainly teaches that the Lord Jesus Christ will unexpectedly return at the end of this present age. Universal and righteous judgment will then be administered, followed by the inauguration of the eternal state. In the meantime, the people of God are to seek, in the Holy Spirit's power, to live each day to the glory of God.

The Position of Israel

It is impossible to avoid considering the position of Israel in any book purporting to deal with the Consummation. The nation past, present and future therefore needs careful review.

Israel in the Old Testament

About 4,000 years ago there was not a Jewish nation, indeed there was not a single Jew! The Lord then called Abram, a descendant of Noah's son, Shem, and told him to go to a land that he would be shown. God initially promised to make him into a great nation and, through him, to bless all the peoples on earth. Abram was later promised that his seed would receive the land of Canaan (Genesis chapter 12).

Abram finally set out for Canaan with his wife who was actually his half-sister, Sarai, and his nephew, Lot. God renewed his promise about the land and also the vast multitude of offspring to be born in process of time (Genesis chapters 13 and 15). In chapter 17, God stressed that the covenant of circumcision must be kept by Abraham (no longer Abram) and his descendants. Sarah (no longer Sarai) and he were to have a 'miracle' son, Isaac, with whom the covenant was to be established.

Ishmael, the son of Abraham and the Egyptian maidservant, Hagar, was not to be the chosen seed but he also would be the father of numberless descendants (Genesis chapters 16 and 25).

In Genesis chapter 28, when Jacob, Isaac's younger son, fled for his life from the anger of his twin brother Esau, God renewed his covenant with him about the land and how all peoples on earth would be blessed through Jacob's offspring.

As their history developed, Jacob, his twelve sons and their families found themselves in Egypt from which God promised to bring them back to Canaan as a great nation (Genesis chapter 46). In fact, the Israelites were in Egypt for over 400 years until rescued by Moses under the providential hand of Almighty God and these details are to be found in the book of Exodus. Without doubt, the key verses which dealt with the nation's relationship to God were to be found in chapter 19:3-8. God stated that if the people obeyed him fully and kept his covenant then they would be his treasured possession out of all the nations. They all responded that they would be obedient to God in everything and this is confirmed in chapter 24. However subsequent history was to give the lie to their commitment.

Exodus records the deliverance from Egypt, the giving of the Ten Commandments together with many other laws dealing with, inter alia, servants, property, social responsibility and sabbaths. Details in respect of the making of the tabernacle, or tent, and its furniture were also provided and the Lord undertook to meet with Moses at the special Ark of the Testimony. Following the very sad affair of the Golden Calf, God stated that he was making a covenant with Israel and called for obedience to his commands as set out in chapter 34. Finally the tabernacle, the furniture and the surrounds were completed and 'the cloud covered the Tent of Meeting and the glory of the Lord filled the tabernacle.' This was described in chapter 40.

The book of Leviticus was concerned with certain types of offerings, for example, the burnt, the sin and the fellowship. Moses' brother Aaron and his sons were ordained as priests and began their ministry. The annual Day of Atonement for sins was also established and it is important to note, at this stage, that the writer of the New Testament letter to the Hebrews drew special attention to this sacrificial system. God again reminded the people that, if they rejected his decrees and violated his covenant, he will bring severe judgment against them. However, as a result of genuine confession and repentance, God promised to remember his covenant and his land (chapter 36).

Numbers included the report of the twelve spies who were sent by Moses to explore the land of Canaan. Only two, Joshua and Caleb, were convinced of victory under God and, as a result, the report of the ten spies was accepted leading to open rebellion from the people. God's judgment was meted out in the forty years of wandering in the desert and not one of those men of twenty years old or more, save Joshua and Caleb, entered Canaan (chapter 14).

There was also in Numbers the interesting story of King Balak of Moab who hired Balaam, the prophet from the Euphrates, to come and curse Israel. In the event, Balaam failed to curse them because Israel was blessed of God. However, around that time, Israel bowed down and worshipped the gods of Moab and God's fierce anger was kindled against the nation and no less than 24,000 died in the plague (Chapter 25).

Deuteronomy means 'repetition of the law', and included Moses recounting the story of the past forty years as Israel was now poised to finally enter and possess the land of promise. Moses, because of his own disobedience, was only permitted to see Canaan from Mount Pisgah and it was Joshua who would actually lead the people into their inheritance. Moses pleaded with the people to obey the Lord and to keep his laws. The worship of false gods and the doing of evil at any stage would ensure God's judgment in their destruction and scattering among other peoples. Moses plainly set out the blessings of obedience and the curses for disobedience (Chapter 28). The Lord predicted that, soon after Moses' death, the people would break the covenant he made with them thus bringing disasters upon them (Chapter 31).

The book of Joshua told how the tribes entered in and possessed a good measure of Canaan. Joshua, towards the end of his life, again reminded the people that if they violated God's covenant and served other gods, they would perish from the land and be destroyed. Once again, the people committed themselves to serving the Lord (Chapters 23 and 24).

The book of Judges made sad reading as the tribes were unable, for whatever reasons, to possess all their inheritance. When they turned from God their enemies prevailed until in repentance they returned to the Lord.

It was a most unsatisfactory episode in the nation's history.

In due course, Eli, the old priest, gave way to Samuel the prophet and later Israel had their first king in Saul only to be replaced by David, 'who enjoyed God's favour' (Acts 7:46). David however was denied the opportunity to build a temple for the Lord and this privilege was given to his own son, Solomon. Nonetheless God promised David that his throne would be established forever (2 Samuel chapter 7). This promise was fulfilled in the Lord Jesus who was and is of the royal line of David. The apostle Peter specifically referred to this fulfilment when he preached at Pentecost as detailed in Acts chapter 2. Jesus, at his resurrection, was made 'both Lord and Christ'.

Disaster however lay ahead for Israel. The Kingdom became divided and it was not too long before the northern section, or the 'Ten Tribes', was carried off into captivity by Assyria, never to return. The people forsook God and, as they had been warned on many occasions, God forsook them. The same situation occurred with regard to the Southern Kingdom, that is, Judah and it was taken into captivity by the Babylonians around 600 BC. After about seventy years, the exile ended, in accordance with God-given prophecy, and some of the nation returned home to rebuild Jerusalem chiefly under the inspiration and guidance of people like Nehemiah and Ezra. The Book of Daniel the prophet is set around this time in Babylon which was later overthrown by the Medo-Persian empire.

Malachi's prophecy is the last book in the Old

Testament and the picture of Judah was as bleak as ever. It all made sorry reading. The blemished sacrifices, the wayward priests and the unfaithful people ensured the righteous condemnation of Almighty God. There was the commitment to the coming of 'the prophet Elijah' to bring about real changes. Failing this, the Lord declared 'I will come and strike the land with a curse'. Nevertheless what remained of the Jewish nation was still resident in the land and, as we shall see, it was crucial that this was the case. There also persisted the small faithful remnant of believers in the coming Messiah and this was also essential to God's purposes. However, as far as God's promised blessing being extended to the other nations, nothing vital had happened. There was failure and the Old Testament actually ended with the word 'curse'.

Israel in the New Testament

For about 400 years since Malachi there was a prophetic silence. It was shattered by the arrival of none other than John the Baptist, the one whom Jesus identified as the 'Elijah' of the New Testament. His message was 'Repent for the kingdom of heaven is near' (Matthew 3:2). John fearlessly declared that fruit worthy of repentance must now be produced by the people. In deliberate language he pointed out to the leaders that Jewish nationality meant nothing to God and that already the axe was laid at the root of the trees - the choice of fine fruit or the fiery furnace (Matthew 3:7-12). Jesus was also to reveal that the hearts of the leaders were far from God (Matthew 15:7-9) and, in one discourse with the Jews, he said that, because of their unbelief, they were not the true seed of faithful Abraham (John 8). The deep sadness of the situation was revealed in John 12:37-43. Unparalleled judgment was thus appearing on the horizon and it was going to engulf the people within a comparatively short period of time. This was the main burden of the prophecy of the Lord to his disciples in Matthew 24, Mark 13 and Luke 21. There is no reference to this particular episode in John's gospel and we shall appreciate the reason in due course.

A little earlier we noted that Jesus came into the world 'in the fulness of time' (Galatians 4:4). It not only was the right time politically and morally, but it was also the proper time historically. God had foretold through the prophet Micah over 700 years earlier that the Messiah, the Ruler, was to be born in Bethlehem in Judah and even Herod and the Jewish leaders were aware of this prophecy (Matthew 2:4-7). The nation had still to be resident in the land for God's Word to be fulfilled. Some years later would have been too late because then Israel had been dispelled from the land by the Romans. However, soon after the birth of Jesus, Bethlehem lost its significance and the Messiah grew up in an out-of-the-way part of the country in Nazareth, which was not even mentioned in the Old Testament. It therefore appeared that the land had served its purpose.

At this stage, it is vital to consider how Jesus regarded his own people Israel and their future. The Gospels provide the information. His ministry was centred on 'The Kingdom' and he proclaimed, like John the Baptist, that, to enter, repentance was essential. As we have briefly mentioned, Jesus knew what awaited the nation. He fearlessly pronounced judgment against towns like Capernaum and Bethsaida (Matthew 11:20-24). In deep concern he wept over the inhabitants of Jerusalem because they were about to miss their day of opportunity and instead reap a harvest of unequalled distress (Matthew 23:33-39). Some commentators have noted that, when preaching in Nazareth, Jesus quoted from Isaiah 61:1,2 and he deliberately omitted the chilling words 'and the day of vengeance of our God'. Jesus fulfilled 'the day of grace' but his removal by the wicked hands of the Jews and the Romans ensured the imminent arrival of 'the day of vengeance'.

Two incidents, at least, have a direct bearing on the subject of Israel. On one occasion, Jesus told a parable about the wicked farmers and their treatment of the owner's servants and ultimately his son (Matthew 21:33-46). The Jewish leaders knew that the message was for them and out of their own mouths they condemned themselves. They would forfeit God's Kingdom and they would also perish. Again, as Jesus went to the cross, he told the women of Jerusalem to weep for themselves and not for him because he knew that the most dreadful judgment was just around the corner (Luke 23:27-31).

What was this catastrophe which was to befall Jerusalem? In Matthew 24 and in the similar passages in Mark and Luke, Jesus warned his disciples of the coming destruction of the city. The cup of God's anger had been steadily filling up in the Old Testament period. The rulers and people had often rebelled against God, they had beaten and killed his prophets and now they were about to murder the incarnate Son of God. This was the generation which would feel the brunt of God's judgment (Matthew 23:33-36).

AD70 was and is etched on the minds of Jew and Gentile alike. History provides the detail of that unparalleled distress and tribulation. The inhabitants expected deliverance from God and this never materialised. What made the tribulation so dreadful was not that it was finally inflicted by Titus and his Roman army, but that the absolute mayhem was perpetrated Jew upon Jew! History also recorded that no Christian perished in this destruction because they heeded the prophecy of Jesus (Luke 21:20,21) and fled to a place called Pella, east of the River Jordan.

It should now be noted that this whole prophecy of great tribulation is not referred to in John's gospel which was written about twenty years or so after the judgment of AD70, thus indicating its relevance to that earlier period of history.

Jesus formed his church on the believing Jewish remnant at the outset and he declared that nothing anywhere could stop its worldwide growth (Matthew 16:18). Before his Ascension and the empowering ministry of the Holy Spirit, the Lord told his followers to witness to him in Jerusalem, in Judaea, in Samaria and to the ends of the earth (Acts 1:8). Gospel blessings were about to break out from the narrow confines of

Judaism. This had rarely happened in Old Testament times. God, however, overlooked this situation but now he commanded all men everywhere to repent because he had appointed not only the day of judgment but also the Judge (Acts 17:30,31). Jesus promised to be with his preaching and teaching church until the end of the age (Matthew 28:19,20) and never did he state or even remotely imply that this strategy would be sidelined or withdrawn. And so the messengers of the cross went out first of all to the Jews and later to the Gentiles, that is, all non-Jews. Peter opened the door of God's Kingdom to both the Jews (Acts 2) and the Gentiles (Acts 10) while Paul, a converted Jew, was pre-eminently God's servant to the Gentiles (Acts 9:15). Jesus had declared that there was only one way to God the Father and he was that exclusive way (John 14:6). Judaism bitterly opposed and persecuted the Christian church, as recorded in the book of Acts, and greater progress was made among the Gentiles. They counted themselves blessed indeed to hear the message of forgiveness of sins and generally they welcomed it with open arms. And if we, Jew or Gentile, know Jesus as our Saviour and Lord, we have simply done the same! The Lord taught that there would only be one flock and one shepherd (John 10:16) and around the throne in glory there is only one company (Revelation 7:13).

Looking back over the ground covered, God's primary purpose in choosing Abraham so long ago was ultimately to bring spiritual blessing to all mankind. In reality, the seed was Christ (Galatians 3:16). The

Jewish people and especially the faithful believing remnant had played their part over the two millennia until Christ came. As Paul surveyed the scene and appreciated the implications of it all, he carefully expounded the message in Galatians (chapters 1-4). The Old Testament dispensation had truly served God's purposes but it was now finished with Christ's coming.

The writer to the Hebrews, generally thought to be one of Paul's colleagues, continually pointed to Jesus the Son of God and showed his total superiority over each aspect of the Old Testament economy - the old shadows and types were gone and gone for ever.

As we read in Chapter 11, the Westminster Abbey of Faith, the patriarch Abraham and all the others had their eyes fixed, not on the temporal or material, but on the eternal country and the eternal city whose builder and maker is God. In full accord with this outlook the Lord, Paul and Peter urge us today to set our hearts, our minds and our affections on things above and not on the things of this earthly scene which are passing away.

Romans - Chapters Nine to Eleven

It is now appropriate to briefly consider Paul's reference to Israel in his letter to the Romans in chapters 9 to 11. This epistle is perhaps to be dated between AD57 and 59 and it was written from Greece as Paul turned his face towards the west. It will be most surprising if the contents are in contrast with what the Lord Jesus or even Paul himself had taught elsewhere. The detailed speech which Stephen gave before the Jewish Sanhedrin should also be kept in focus (Acts 7). The Jews had received the law but had disobeyed it. They had always resisted the Holy Spirit and now they had murdered the Son of God.

At Calvary, we see most clearly the sovereignty of God and the responsibility of men. Peter fearlessly declared that Jesus was put to death by wicked hands and yet this was all in the set purpose of God (Acts 2:23).

Chapter 9 tells us of God's sovereignty in every respect. As far as Israel is concerned, not all who are descended from Israel are the true descendants of Abraham. It is not the natural children who are God's children but only the believing remnant, the children of the promise. Israel sought to pursue a law of righteousness, a way of works and had basically failed to put their faith and trust in God. This totally conforms to our earlier findings. (Note also 2:17-29).

In Chapter 10, Paul emphatically declares Christ is the end of the law so that God's righteousness is available for everyone, Jew or Gentile, who believes and calls upon God. Man's righteousness is always totally unacceptable to God. There is only God's way of salvation and once again this teaching is in line with what we have previously considered.

Paul, in chapter 11, refers to the believing remnant of which he is a part, chosen by God's grace. Because of the nation's hardening, the Gentiles have come into blessing and, if the Jews do not persist in unbelief, God is waiting to receive and bless all who repent and turn in faith to him.

It was always God's will that the blessing of Abraham would spread out into all the world to incorporate the Gentiles. There were however questions about it - in what way or on what basis would the Gentiles be included ? Paul makes it abundantly clear in Ephesians 3:3-7 that in the church the Gentiles are to enjoy, and do enjoy a status and position of complete and absolute equality with the believing Jews. They belong to the same body, they have the same access to God through prayer and the atonement purchased by Christ as do the Jews. (The church is not a Jewish or a Gentile one but is the Christian church - it is truly 'the Israel of God'. There is only one 'olive tree').

Verse 26 reads 'And so all Israel will be saved'. Commentators have long differed on the exact meaning of Paul's words and it is therefore unwise to be dogmatic. It may mean that, in the future, increasing numbers of Jews will come to personally trust in Jesus as Messiah and Lord. In our studies there has been nothing indicated to prevent such a joyful happening. God is sovereign and the coming years may well usher in a period of great blessing among Jews and Gentiles before the consummation.

In his doxology Paul stresses that the knowledge and judgments of God are deep and unsearchable (11:33). This clearly reminds us that we do not have all the answers and that wisdom dictates we leave matters in the loving hands of the only wise God.

Our responsibility is to pray, to give or to go in the Lord's Name to share in the extension of God's growing kingdom in a worldwide context. Whatever nation we are concerned about as individuals, it is not of crucial importance so long as we are obedient to God's will as far as we are aware of it. His love in Christ reaches out into the whole world and there is no partiality with the Lord. Jesus commissioned his church to go out to serve him to the ends of the earth. He promised to be with them and with us to the very end of the age at which time He will return.

The Land of Palestine

The state of Israel was proclaimed on 14th May 1948 and after the Six Day War in 1967 there was, inter alia, a united Jerusalem. As we conclude our study of Israel, it is only proper that we review the current situation.

There are two main views about these comparatively recent events. The first claims that the return of the Jews to Palestine is in fulfilment of Old Testament prophecies and accordingly heralds the Return of Christ in the not-too-distant future. (Not a few writers however take the view that, for example, the later prophecies of Zechariah have generally found their fulfilment in the first Advent of Jesus and subsequent history). The other viewpoint, which is not so well known, states that those prophecies were given in respect of the exile in Babylon and were actually fulfilled when the people returned to Jerusalem in the period of Ezra and Nehemiah. They would claim there is therefore no prophecy relating to this return of the Jews to Palestine which started almost fifty years ago.

The nation of Israel is now well established in Palestine but with less land than it held in the golden days of David and Solomon. It is most unlikely that their territory will increase and it will rather tend to decrease as Israel 'trades land for peace' with the Arabs both inside and outside its borders. The big issue in the coming days for the Middle Eastern countries will be the sufficient reserves of water, and, as a result, various arrangements will no doubt be made among the interested parties.

There is therefore the choice of viewpoint about the recent return of Israel to Palestine. The contents of this chapter together with the wide discussion of the Second Advent need to be taken into account. It must again be stressed that nothing has been taken away from the Jews as individuals because God's loving concern reaches out to everyone.

Jesus prophesised that Jerusalem would be trampled on by the Gentiles until the times of the Gentiles are fulfilled (Luke 21:24). However, while confirming that salvation came by means of the Jews, he declared that those who worship God are to do so in spirit and in truth. In this statement Jesus also set aside the earlier significance of venues such as Samaria and Jerusalem (John 4:19-24).

It is vital however to reiterate that, whatever the future, we do not know the date of the Return of Christ. God has provided, in the meantime, only one message for the church to proclaim until the end.

Conclusion

God's concern is for all mankind with whom he desires intimate spiritual fellowship. Our sin and rebellion have however to be faced and dealt with. God chose

Abraham and the nation of Israel, through whom he taught what he required, with the ultimate act of providing salvation in Jesus for all nations.

The Old Testament indicated that, as a whole, Israel failed to please God but he ensured that there was always the faithful believing remnant. God fulfilled his promises and Jesus lived, died and rose again so that the gospel of love and grace could be proclaimed to the end of time. The Holy Spirit empowered the church, comprised of believing Jews and Gentiles, and, over the years, multitudes have been received into God's kingdom and family. In the future, which is totally in God's control, increased numbers of Jews and Gentiles may joyfully trust in the Lord Jesus and they, in turn, go out to witness to others until the consummation.

Conclusion

Death is an unavoidable appointment and as such we approach it in various ways. On the face of it, some ignore its claims although realising it will not go away. Their motto is: 'Eat, drink and be merry for tomorrow we die'. Some do their utmost to delay the Grim Reaper by adopting proven health and fitness techniques. A few even provide finance to have their frail bodies specially treated, hopefully to return to this earthly scene for a short visit to sample the anticipated medical improvements in fighting mortality.

Most people however are persuaded that death does not end everything. Many in this category, especially in the East, hold beliefs about reincarnation, absorption into the universe and similar ideas. The Christian has definite views on the future resurrection and judgment and these have already been discussed in earlier chapters.

A philosophy of death is a prerequisite to one for life and it makes no sense whatsoever to have an outlook on life without having a reasoned view about death.

Our difficulty is that we have become all too accustomed to life to fail to see it for the miracle it truly is. We have witnessed a continual growth in population over thousands of years. Today we know more about ourselves and our surroundings than we have ever known before and this knowledge will further increase, for example, in technology, communications, commerce and space. Nevertheless we are all individuals, each one is unique, each is valued, each is a miracle. Assuming no very elderly reader of this book, 100 years ago not one of us was living! That we are here today is the reality, the miracle. It is the concept that we definitely continue to exist after what we call 'death', which ought to be commonplace, to be the norm.

Death is, in effect, the open gateway to another sphere of unbounded existence. Life is the 'real thing' with death no more than a blip. The Creator, on whom all may totally rely, declares that he is not the God of the dead but of the living (Mark 12:26,27). Elsewhere he states that not one sparrow falls to the ground without his knowledge. This even includes the one which was given away for free as part of a bargain sale! That the very hairs of our head are counted certainly should make us catch our breath (Luke 12:4-7).

Evolution is inevitably a belief without hope and this is admitted by its devotees. If life arose in the first place by a freak accident then clearly today is all there is and tomorrow is oblivion.

We can feel the anguish and uncertainty of the well known Darwinist, Dr. Peter Atkins, when considering his greatest mystery of all, he said 'The emergence of something from nothing without external intervention, and the stumbling of that something into the capacity to comprehend itself.' This is the sorry plight of those who persist in going their own way instead of submitting to their Creator (Romans 8:5-8).

Can we conclusively prove that death ends everything? The evolutionist is honest enough to admit that his belief may well be found wanting in the final reckoning. There thus exists the dire reality of personal judgment when, as the apostle Paul states, the fire will test each man's work of what quality (not quantity) it is (1 Corinthians 3:11-13).

On the other hand, the true believer in the Lord Jesus has 'the best of both worlds' and there is no doubt or argument about it. In this age, even in opposition or persecution, he enjoys a deep peace, real purpose with the certain hope of unending life in the age to come. If his faith in the present and the future somehow turns out to be misplaced he loses nothing. If however the non-believer of whatever persuasion makes the wrong decision he loses everything - eternally. Thankfully we are still in the day of opportunity and the way to life in the Father is wide open for us through Jesus, the Son of God.

The Christian can claim no superiority over anyone else. Rather he freely admits that he is 'a sinner saved by God's grace'. He is the one who recognised his need of forgiveness when it was drawn to his attention. He rejoices in God's salvation which comprehensively deals with his past, present and future. He is fully aware that this epoch of time is inexorably drawing to a close. An eternal reality will be his to share with his loving Lord in company with the countless multitudes of the redeemed from every age and nation. 'Is there anything too hard for the Lord?' (Genesis 18:11-15). Jesus said, 'With God, all things are possible' (Mark 10:26,27).

In the final analysis, the fact that humanity exists at

all is claimed as the proof of evolution or scientific naturalism. When pressed, the Darwinist openly admits that evolution is a faith. There is no genuine evidence to support it (the observed evidence actually contradicts evolution) and yet he states that to believe in special creation is unthinkable. The alternative to the Creator's revelation in Genesis is to rely on the assumption that Nothing created Something out of Nothing. It is now left to the reader to carefully decide which of the alternatives is the less incredible.

Appendix I

Millennial Considerations

In this section we take the opportunity to consider the key topic of the Millennium which has been variously interpreted in the study of biblical prophecy. It is also essential that the contents of some of the earlier chapters are kept very much in mind.

The Millennium, which literally means 'one thousand years', only occurs six times in the whole of the bible! References are in Revelation 20, regarded by practically every commentator as the most difficult book and chapter in the Word of God. The apostle Peter also referred to a thousand years, in God's sight, as being like one day and vice versa (2 Peter 3:8). This is taken to mean that, as the Almighty is outside time and space, he is not limited in any way as we mortals are. It also needs to be stressed, at this stage, that there are even variations within each prophetic viewpoint and it is not intended to consider them.

Historic Premillennialism

Advocates of Historic Premillennialism generally claim that the church, at the hands of a future Antichrist, will endure a Great Tribulation of seven years after which the Lord Jesus will return to reign on the earth. He will establish his kingdom of peace and righteousness for one thousand literal years during which the ministry of the church will be abundantly blessed. This ministry is said to be identified in the Old Testament prophecies, for example, in Isaiah 2:2-4. 11:1-10. and Micah 4:1-5. (Some commentators however regard such prophecies as relevant to the spiritual blessing Jesus brought at his first Advent. It is also clear that one does relate to the eternal state and not to a Millennium, as indicated in Isaiah 65:17-25).

At the end of the Millennium, Satan the deceiver will be released from his enforced captivity, he will raise a rebellion which will be overthrown by God (Revelation 20). The Great White Throne judgment will then be set up followed by the ushering in of the New heavens and the New earth. While the Great White Throne judgment, which is universal, has already been discussed, it will be necessary to review such themes as the Antichrist, the Great Tribulation and the Resurrection in more detail.

Dispensationalism

The Dispensational viewpoint on prophecy is both similar and dissimilar to Historic Premillennialism.

This school teaches that the church (the bride of Christ) will actually escape the future Tribulation by being caught away, that is, the Rapture (there is a possible reference in 1 Thessalonians 4). The church will receive its judgment at that time and thus avoid that of the Great White Throne.

The Millennium will again last for one thousand literal years and it will be a period of great blessing through the ministry, not of the church, but of the Jews. It is also taught that there will be a period of great salvation during the Tribulation when, although the Holy Spirit has been withdrawn with the church, another gospel, 'the gospel of the Kingdom' will be preached by a Jewish remnant (some claim the 144,000 of Revelation 7). While this general view appears to be in conflict with the teaching of a universal judgment (Revelation 20:11-15, Matthew 25:31-46, Acts 10:42, Romans 14:10-12), it will also be essential to examine the concepts of the Rapture and the 'other gospel'. In the Dispensational system, Jesus comes before the Tribulation and also before the Millennium, that is, the belief is 'double pre' - pre-tribulational and pre-millennial.

Amillennialism

The Amillennial school adopts the view that there are insufficient grounds in scripture to support a future millennium of worldwide peace and they assert that the 'thousand years' in Revelation 20 covers the lengthy period from the First to the Second Advent during which time the gospel is proclaimed and is reasonably successful through the gracious and powerful ministry of the Holy Spirit. Most adherents anticipate, like the other schools, a tough time just prior to the Second Advent which leads into the universal 'Great Assize'. Jesus, as previously discussed, referred to 'this age and the next' and the writer to the Hebrews in chapter 1 actually alludes to the first coming of Jesus in terms of 'these last days'.

Postmillennialism

The Postmillennial viewpoint is quite interesting in that it anticipates a lengthy period of blessing and peace before, and not after, the Return of Christ. Adherents stress that it is unwise to take the figure of 'one thousand years' literally in a book full of numbers, pictures and symbols which are clearly not meant to be taken in such a fashion. This view therefore expects a period probably well in excess of one thousand years of great blessing through the preaching of the gospel. Opponents pessimistically have claimed that the scriptures teach that things are to deteriorate rather than improve. However, the Postmillennial view stresses that, in context, Paul was referring to the general situation in Timothy's own day and not specially to the present time (2 Timothy 3:1-5). Indeed the progress of the gospel since the first century to date has been phenomenal and is in accord with Postmillennialism. And, if the Almighty so wills it, there is absolutely nothing to prevent further increase as all kinds of barriers come down and opportunities arise in our global village. Did not the Lord himself refer to real advance by reference to the tiny mustard seed which is outward growth and to the pervasive leaven that is inward ? He also declared that it was impossible to stop the progress of his church (Matthew 16:18). Jesus also has received all power in heaven and on earth (Matthew 28:18). It is of note that it was not 'some power' but 'all power' and Jesus surely cannot receive any more because he has it all already !

Summary

In summary at this stage, it is clear that two prophetic schools are perhaps reasonably close to each other, that is, Amillennialism and Postmillennialism, the real difference being one of degree. The Postmillennialist anticipates even greater long-term blessing as the gospel wins its way into the hearts and lives of the nations while most, but not all, Amillennialists are not prepared to fully accept that scenario. They carefully note that a future Millennium never appears in the plain teaching of the Lord Jesus or Paul or Peter. Indeed there is basically only one reference to a Millennium in one book, that is, Revelation and it is considered to be far too weak and uncertain to secure any weight of doctrine.

The Dispensational school has been linked most closely with the popular Scofield Bible in which the views of leading adherents are actually included as explanatory footnotes to the scriptures. This is not a recommended practice because the unwary may consider that the footnotes are as inspired as the Word of God and this is definitely not the case. Dispensationalism which,to an extent, is an extreme form of Premillennialism, is a comparatively recent viewpoint and is to be dated around 1830. However part of it may be traced back to a Jesuit monk, named Ribera, who developed the futurist interpretation around 1580 to show that the Pope could not possibly be the Antichrist. The Dispensational view has been in decline in recent decades as former adherents have openly admitted that it is scripturally unsound.

Are There Two Gospels ?

Many may well be startled by such a strange question because they are unaware that Dispensationalists teach that there are two gospels for two different times! There is 'the gospel of the grace of God' which is being and will be preached until the Rapture after which 'the gospel of the Kingdom' will be proclaimed by the Jews. Such a view appears to be contrary not only to our earlier studies but to the general teaching of the Word of God and therefore it should ring alarm bells for its adherents. It should be noted that when Paul refers to his ministry in Acts (20:24-27) he uses both of the above expressions to describe one and the same message. Paul stressed that there was only one gospel (Galatians 1:6-9) and in the book of Revelation we read of the 'eternal' gospel (14:6).

The Rapture

The bible certainly teaches about the 'Rapture' but it is totally different from the way in which the Dispensational school regards it. Most, if not all Dispensationalists, believe that there will be a 'secret Rapture', that is, Christians will one day simply disappear all over the world because God has changed them and taken them home to glory before the Tribulation. However, as previously noted, a relevant verse in 1 Thessalonians 4:16 is arguably the noisiest one in the bible! To make matters worse, this viewpoint requires a further short succession of Raptures ! Those accepting the so-called 'kingdom gospel' during the Tribulation would need to be raptured or changed in preparation for the Millennium. A similar occurrence would be required at the end of the Millennium to enable those receiving the gospel to be ready for the eternal state. The scriptures only teach one Rapture for those actually living at the time of the Second Advent. To require a duplicate and a triplicate are clear indications that the Dispensational theory is not securely based in scripture.

The Resurrection

As with the Rapture, the same type of difficulty applies to the Dispensationalist view of the resurrection. In fact, the Dispensational school is compelled to consider possibly four future resurrections ! Believers who die during the Great Tribulation need to be resurrected to participate in the Millennium. Similarly, those who believe and die during the Millennium will require to be resurrected at the end of it in order to enter into the eternal state. There is also some doubt as to exactly when the Old Testament saints will obtain their resurrection. Are they included when the church is raptured before the Tribulation or are they separately raised ? Finally, there is the resurrection of the 'wicked dead' of all ages to face the Great White Throne judgment.

As noted earlier, the bible consistently teaches only one future resurrection and judgment. These are singular events with everyone in attendance.

Some have suggested that the expression, 'the first resurrection', possibly indicates a special one occurring before the general resurrection (Revelation 20)! This expression however needs to be contrasted with another one, 'the second death', which means eternal separation from God for the unrepentant. In context, 'the first resurrection' refers to believers who willingly die and suffer for the faith and who now reign in glory with their Lord.

The Great Tribulation

Those who maintain a future Tribulation of seven years seek to find a basis for this view in Daniel chapter 9:24-27. There is an abundance of literature available on the subject of Daniel's seventieth week, that is, a period actually reckoned to be one week of years, thus giving a total of seven years.

Dispensationalists teach that Daniel's seventieth week has become detached from the other sixty nine so that it has still to occur in the future ! They also insist that the six-fold purpose (9:24) does not relate to the Messiah and the accomplishment at Calvary. Traditional scholars are most unhappy with the manner in which Dispensationalists treat these verses. When 'the prince of preachers', Charles Spurgeon, preached on verse 24, he related it to Calvary and did not even find it necessary to refer to the distinctive Dispensational treatment. It should be recalled that when Jesus spoke about the coming distress and tribulation on Jerusalem, he referred particularly to Daniel's prophecy (Matthew 24:15). In the light of the events of those days and also Paul's specific reference in 1 Thessalonians 2:14-16, numerous scholars are of the view that the Great Tribulation occurred around AD70. It was of course a prophecy when Jesus alluded to it about AD30.

There is also a reference in Revelation where those

who have come out of 'great tribulation' are said to have washed their robes and made them white in the blood of the Lamb (7:14). Dispensationalists usually claim that this relates to the future Tribulation. If so, how could these people have washed their robes in the blood of the Lamb when, during the Great Tribulation, Dispensationalists teach that another gospel with 'no blood' is to be preached ? This is yet another difficulty for this prophetic school and it does underline the unsuitability of building doctrine on a book like Revelation.

In overall terms, it is unrealistic to limit opposition and tribulation to a particular place and time. Suffering has been and will continue to be the portion of those who seek to live godly lives.

The Antichrist

Everyone has heard of the 'Antichrist' - but who is he and when is he expected ? Even as I write, some people in the former USSR are expecting Antichrist or even the end of the world this very weekend!

It will perhaps come as a big surprise to most that there are only four references to the word 'antichrist' in the whole of the bible! Other mentions are often claimed but these are by inference only and they are speculative and not definitive.

A study of the four references (1 John 2:18,22. 4:3. 2 John 7) teaches that any person or spirit or system which denies the deity and humanity of Christ is actually anti-Christ. This was the situation not only in John's day but in every generation since that time.

It should now have become clear that there seems to be no genuine biblical evidence to support the future coming of a special antichrist. The Lord Jesus prophesied the coming of 'false Christs' before the destruction of Jerusalem in AD70 (Luke 21:8) and history records that such events occurred. Some however suggest that 'the little horn' of Daniel 8 is or represents a future antichrist. This is no more than presumption and commentators widely accept that 'the little horn' is to be identified with Antiochus Epiphanes whose atrocities against the Jews were well documented around 168 BC.

Nowhere in the gospels, the Acts or in the epistles is there even one reference to a future antichrist and this total absence is most significant. Some dubiously suggest that Paul's 'Man of Sin' in 2 Thessalonians 2 is the possible future antichrist. However this notion once again is really no more than speculation. In context, Paul was alluding to a specific situation about which he had spoken when he was with the Thessalonians. Things were actually developing before their very eyes, the temple in Jerusalem was still standing and it requires a lot of imagination to assume that such events will somehow occur at a time which is even today still in the future. Commentators have mixed opinions on this unusual portion and it is foolhardy to build any sort of major structure on such an uncertain foundation.

Brief reference must now be made to the book of The Revelation and, once again, it is noted that it contains no actual reference to antichrist. The book is largely written in symbol and code and is to be categorised as 'apocalyptic', or vision, like some of the book ofDaniel. It gave and does give tremendous encouragement to the persecuted Christians not only of the apostle John's time but also to believers down the ages and in our own day. The clear message is that we can be and are 'more than conquerors through Christ Jesus who loved us' (Romans 8:36,37). Commentators generally admit that it is unwise to seek to build a doctrine or scheme of future events on the book of Revelation because of the nature of this type of literature. There is also the real danger of seeking to find a particular view to the exclusion of all other legitimate ones, and then dogmatically imposing it on what are the more obvious verses of scripture, thus distorting or negating their meaning.

Finally, the bible states that Jesus is now seated at the right hand of the throne of God, waiting until all his enemies are made his footstool (Psalm 110:1). Paul declares that the last enemy to be destroyed is death (1 Corinthians 15:26). Revelation 20:14 clearly teaches that death is to be cast into the lake of fire only at the time of the final judgment. It is surely inconsistent with scripture for Premillennialists and Dispensationalists to expect the Return of Christ one thousand years or more before the Great Assize because it is only then that death will finally be destroyed.

Conclusion

Discussion surrounding the Millennium and related topics has often been to the forefront especially in some branches of the Christian church. The Lord's teaching and that of his apostles appeared to be clear and consistent in respect of the Second Advent and the Judgment and yet somehow different approaches have been developed over the years. On review, there is no compelling argument to depart from the generally accepted teaching of the scriptures. The risen Lord Jesus commissioned his invincible church, comprised of believing Jews and Gentiles, and promised to be with them until the very end of the age.

Appendix II

The Age of the Earth

'How old is the earth?' is a fascinating question which regularly raises its head and generates lots of discussion.

Had this question been asked about 200 years ago, the answer for the earth's age would have been about 5,800 years. Archbishop James Ussher of Armagh, Ireland had published a start date of 4004 BC in 1650 by basically adding up the years given in the genealogies of the Old Testament. This result was generally accepted by churchmen and scientists alike.

When this question is considered today, the answer given is totally different. Current scientific thinking indicates an initial 'Big Bang' about 15 billion years ago with an earth, moon and sun formation to be dated about 4.6 billion years ago. To admit there is a difference in the two answers is something of an understatement.

The figure of almost 5 billion years is widely referred to in the media and taught in the education system so that almost everyone has heard that the earth is very old. This is accepted by all concerned including the majority of Christians. Indeed to suggest any other approach or date is to be very much frowned upon.

Let us briefly examine the two dates. Using Ussher's

assessment of 4004 BC, this means that the earth is now about 6,000 years old and some argue for such a date. They claim that the genealogies were carefully compiled and thus the result is reliable. On the other hand, it is fair to state that this view does not attract wide support because of several factors.

Scholars have indicated that, in their judgment, the genealogies were not meant to be taken as complete because there are omissions when it is possible to compare one with another. There is also the structure, for example, from Abraham to David, from David to the Exile and from then to Christ (Matthew 1:17). There are 14 generations in each section no doubt indicating a special arrangement. The genealogies were not strictly provided to be added up by means of simple arithmetic but were primarily to show the line of descent or inheritance. Indeed it is possible that some individuals did not warrant a mention in a line of succession for whatever reason. Commentators also suggest that the word translated 'father' may also mean 'ancestor' and therefore any straightforward addition of ages would understate the end result.

One other aspect must be taken into consideration and this relates to the history of the land of Egypt. Much has been learnt about this country in recent years and it is now widely agreed there is reliable information going back, without a break, to around 3100 BC. This of course means that the Noachic flood must have occurred prior to this time thus indicating that Ussher's date of 4004 BC is too soon and should be set much earlier. It should however be noted that current Egyptian dating may be overstated by at least 300 years. Some experts are currently of the view that there is a measure of duplication in the records between 1200 BC and 700 BC.

We have previously stated that the Word of God is totally concerned with the redemption of mankind after the havoc caused by the Fall and, to that extent, dating is not of importance. Indeed, from the details available in the bible, which is by far the oldest reliable book in the world, it is impossible to give a firm date for Adam. It should therefore be stressed that any dates provided are no more than 'ball park' figures as other information may yet be uncovered which would render them untenable. We should never close our eyes to the possibility of other discoveries and this caution applies equally to creationists and to evolutionists.

And yet everyone likes a date or dates with which to be able to agree or disagree! A possible date for the flood in the days of Noah may be about 7,000 or 8,000 years ago. It is however much more difficult to put a date on Adam but some have reckoned him to be about 10,000 to 15,000 years ago at this state of our knowledge. In any event, from the bible record, Adam is not to be dated millions of years ago. Indeed, an estimate of 20,000 years ago may be excessive.

Before considering the suggested ancient date for the earth the following matters should be noted. Firstly, history as we know it only goes back several thousand years and this gives much cause for thought. Secondly, as discussed earlier, the mammoth only became extinct about 3,000 or 3,500 years ago, that is, around the time of the building of the pyramids in Egypt. Finally, it must be emphasised that the Lord Jesus placed Adam and Eve inextricably with the creation - and he should know! Concerning Abel it was also stated that his righteous blood was the first to be shed on earth since the beginning of the world (Matthew 23:35. Luke 11:50,51).

Darwinism, let us never forget, is anti-God of the bible and blatantly removes the Creator from his throne and gives the glory to the creature. The evolutionist tends to place a zero or nil value on the life of a human being while God places an infinite value on such a person (Luke 9:25). The bible says about such futile thinking: 'Although they claimed to be wise, they became fools' (Romans 1:22) and believers in the Lord Jesus should not be associated with such a view in any shape or form.

The Big Bang was and is and will only ever be a theory even if it is revised. When God is left out of the reckoning, some scheme or notion must be developed to explain what we see around us. Any explanation is better than none especially as no one was around at the time to witness the origins. It defies our mental capacity to really appreciate millions and billions of years and yet the numbers are related in such a glib manner as if we had the ability to comprehend them. In 1993, for example, there was a BBC TV programme about 'Ghost Dinosaurs' and the incredible sight was that of a group of American palaeontologists in the Gobi Desert picking up remains on the surface or just below and casually dating them at countless millions of years old. Compare this with the work of archaeologists who have to dig down into the ground for many metres and yet have only travelled back in time a thousand or a few thousand years at most!

It is generally thought that the universe is expanding although some scientists are of the opinion that it is actually contracting! If it is expanding, yesterday it was a little smaller and it was even smaller a year ago. By means of this backward extrapolation the universe is thought to be contracted to a single point of 'explosion' about 15 billion years ago. So runs the theory.

The question to be asked is how this material or nugget arose in the first place and of course the hypothesis states that it really just had to be there - Abracadabra! Then apparently about 10 billion years ago, the first stars began to form from the cooling gas in the young universe. Almost four billion years ago, life is supposed to have formed - by accident. In 1993, in the TV documentary, international scientists expressed several theories which largely contradicted each other and they were unable to agree how life got underway. Life only produces life - it is not produced from non-life.

Many scientists today do not accept the Big Bang scenario and it is of course out of step with the scriptures. There are various problems with the theory which are rarely covered in the relevant literature. For example, what ignited the Big Bang ? In what natural way can the formation of intricate planets, stars and galaxies be explained from an explosion ? Life should have developed everywhere in the evolving universe - where is everybody ? Indeed, where are all the missing neutrinos which should be flooding earth as a result of the sun's fusion process? Calculations indicate that the control of the Big Bang would have had to be so infinitely precise as to be impossible in purely natural terms.

There are many other methods which have been adopted in the measurement of the age of the earth and these do not receive much publicity because they indicate a much younger earth than five billion years. There now follows samples of other approaches.

Firstly, the measured rate of generation of Carbon 14 in the atmosphere exceeds the rate of extinction or decay by as much as 38%. It was calculated that equilibrium would have been established in about 30,000 years. On this basis the earth's atmosphere may be dated at very much less than 30,000 years.

Secondly, if the earth is really as old as claimed by the Darwinians, there should be many billions of tons of radiogenic helium in the atmosphere. In fact, there is comparatively little and a straightforward calculation gives a maximum age for the earth of about 175,000 years. This figure could be grossly overstated because there may have been helium 4 to start with and also there may be helium entry from the sun's activity.

Thirdly, when the first landing on the moon was being planned, it was thought that, because of the assumed ancient age of the moon, there would literally be a sea of dust into which the lunar craft would disappear. In the event, there was little or no dust thus indicating a comparatively recent creation. This topic has however been much discussed and scientists have made major adjustments on dust-fall calculations.

Moon probes have also indicated that it is still cooling down and this confirms that the moon is nowhere near as old as the theory currently suggests. Such matters need to be openly investigated, reported upon and not kept mainly under wraps.

Finally, calculations have been made with regard to the amount of nickel content of meteoric dust dissolved in the earth's seas and oceans. It is estimated that this level could have been transported there in under 10,000 years. In a similar manner, when the salinity of the oceans is measured, the level of salt content is achieved in a time very much less than five billion years. This particular answer may well be overstated because of the impact of the usual three 'unknowns' - the position at the outset, the constancy or otherwise of the annual rate and the influence of outside factors.

Those who accept a recent creation viewpoint claim that the above and other methods indicate a young earth and not an ancient one. As far as the general population is concerned, it is only the dates which may support an ancient earth which are carefully circulated in the public domain. There is abundant literature on this topic which is referred to at the end of the book. It is confidently asserted by creationists that their hard evidence for a recent creation is much greater than that for an ancient one. However it appears unlikely that scientists will be able to settle the issue because there are still many unknowns. At the end of the day, it does come down to one's mind-set. It is claimed that, as already discussed, the bible points to a young earth created by the Almighty and not to an ancient one which is linked to fallible evolutionary notions.

It should of course be noted that there are Christians who are opposed to both evolution and theistic evolution and yet they believe in an ancient creation. Some also attempt to see a gap between Genesis chapter 1 verses 1 and 2 in which a vast age may be inserted but commentators generally look unfavourably at such a treatment of the text. If nothing transpired in this lengthy period, there is no genuine need to maintain such a gap. If however they adopt the view that there was activity in this period, it runs counter to the scripture which declares that Adam and Eve were created at the beginning.Others favour the view that the 'days' of Genesis chapter 1 relate to long periods of time. There are also admitted drawbacks to this scheme which has no scriptural support and has been rebutted in recent years by former advocates, for example, the well known geologist, R. Davis Young of Calvin College,USA.

It is also important to record that some Christians tend to the view that the early chapters of Genesis are to be regarded as a parable or allegory or something similar. Once again, they have been unduly influenced by evolutionary opinion that the earth is billions of years old and so they formulate a view of scripture to accommodate this assumption. (In general it is unwise to link biblical interpretation to current scientific theories because, from experience, they are prone to later amendment and even rejection).

There are obvious difficulties with this approach. If,

for example, early Genesis is a parable, what does it mean? God created the sun and the moon - what do they represent? God created the fish and the animals - what do they stand for? The Creator made human beings - what do they represent if not human beings? The Lord Jesus and the apostles generally treated Genesis as historical narrative and there is no scope at all for regarding it as parable. Such a view is not only without foundation but it is in opposition to the clear teaching of the Word of God.

At the heart of the matter, there are two distinctive approaches to the dating of the earth. There is the firm belief which has persisted for thousands of years that God's Word teaches a comparatively recent creation in which humans in God's image featured right from the start. The other view is that life started totally by accident billions of years ago, there has been gradual evolution in the intervening ages and that God is superfluous. For the follower of the Lord Jesus, there is really only the one view without any need for compromise. The choice is clear - the scriptures or the opinions of sinful man. As our trust for this life and the life to come is in God alone, it is unreasonable that we can doubt his revelation about origins especially when it is so much in accord with observed evidence.

Evolution is no more than an ingenious idea - if there is no Creator! Basic commonsense challenges us that there is a Supreme Being and it is over to the Darwinist to prove conclusively there is no God - this he very wisely admits he cannot do. It has therefore become fashionable for him to claim that incredulity about ourselves and our surroundings does not of itself prove there is a Creator. This is a sleight of hand to avoid facing reality. There have been many clear indications in this book of a holy and active God. We still await one genuine fact to substantiate the evolutionary belief. There has been no shortage of ideas and passion - only an absence of evidence.

Dinosaur Dilemma

Today, dinosaurs are all the rage! ‘Dinomania’ has become established and has been successfully exploited in the commercial world. As we shall discover, however, dinosaurs may provide a vital clue to assessing the age of the earth.

Evolutionists are most insistent that, based on uniformitarian ideas, dinosaurs uniquely ruled the earth from about 220 to 65 million years ago. At that stage, they mysteriously became extinct while, surprisingly, other newer and weaker creatures somehow managed to survive. Various speculations have been made to account for their demise, the most convincing one being related to turbulent waters which effectively covered them (and other creatures), or most of them, with sediments and thus provided ideal conditions for their fossilisation.

In recent years, the dinosaur has been possibly the flagship of evolution belief as most people seem to accept ancient dates for these ‘terrible lizards’ or reptiles, some of which were no more than the size of chickens. Indeed, if these dates can be shown to be wrong or open to serious doubt then, effectively,

Darwinism is further exposed to be the fiction which many believe it to be.

There are several lines of evidence which strongly suggest that dinosaurs and their marine counterparts, the plesiosaurs, are of more recent origin and actually co-existed with human beings.

During 1993, a Channel 4 TV series about dinosaurs, from an evolutionary viewpoint, showed an illustration which referred to a large creature called 'behemoth', described in obvious eye-witness detail in the Old Testament book of Job in chapter 40. Behemoth was portrayed as one of the big plant-eating dinosaurs and yet Job is to be dated only several thousand years ago (this creature is definitely not an elephant or hippopotamus as some writers suggest). Leviathan is probably another type of dinosaur which is described in detail in Job chapter 41. There is also an awesome description of leviathan in the first century AD book of *The Shepherd of Hermas* where it was said to be about 30 metres in length.

An article in 'Science' (July 1993) told of a graduate student in Montana, USA, who, under the microscope, noticed visible blood cells threaded through part of the bone of a Tyrannosaurus Rex. She felt that this was impossible if dinosaurs really became extinct about 70 million years ago. Such a discovery surely places dinosaurs thousands and not millions of years ago.

In the overall context, dinosaur eggs have been recently found in China and have been dated at 80 million years ago! In view of all the dreadful ravages that have beset the planet, for example, floods, meteorites and earthquakes, it is unreasonable to presume that eggs could have survived for such a period - for perhaps a comparatively short time but hardly for endless millions of years!

If dinosaurs had really evolved, we would naturally expect to discover fossils that were part-dinosaur or which could be classed as intermediates or links. There is no such evidence which confirms our conclusion when we earlier examined evolution theory. The fossil record clearly indicates that dinosaurs have always been dinosaurs - they certainly did not evolve from anything into something different. They were uniquely designed as dinosaurs.

In 1961, in Alaska, a petroleum geologist found fresh, unmineralised bones which he assumed were bison bones. However, about twenty years later, the bones were authenticated as belonging to a duck-billed dinosaur and the deposit also contained the bones of other large and small dinosaurs. This find presented a dilemma to the scientists of the universities of California and Alaska - if the dinosaurs really lived 70 million years ago, how could they have remained in such a fresh condition ? They were certainly not preserved by cold weather because then the climate was much warmer as was indicated by the redwood trees which could still be sawn and burned.

A young Inuit (Canadian Eskimo), working with scientists from Newfoundland, also found fresh, unfossilised dinosaur bones on Bylot Island. This occurred in 1987 and, once again, the assumed millions of years simply vanish in the light of the evidence.

During 1993, some researchers at Newcastle University were able to isolate a protein from fossil dinosaur bones. Such an achievement was most puzzling because protein is unable to last for lengthy periods of time. Added to this, some scientists from Columbus, Ohio, USA, were actually able to date dinosaur bones by means of the radioactive carbon 14 method. According to theory, amounts of carbon 14 cannot exist beyond 40,000 - 50,000 years. The mere presence of carbon 14 in dinosaur bones proves that they are only thousands and not millions of years old.

Many historical records worldwide going back over the past few thousand years bear eloquent testimony to the fact that dinosaurs, dragons and plesiosaurs have co-existed with homo sapiens sapiens.Some explorers and scientists cautiously admit that dinosaurs may even exist today, for example, in the swamps and rainforests of the Congo. After all, it was claimed that Stegadon was extinct for 1 million years until two bull mammoths were discovered in a remote part of Nepal in 1993 by John Blashford-Snell!

There is now abundant evidence available to claim that dinosaurs ought to be dated in the comparatively recent past. Once again, as with the Piltdown Man scandal earlier this century, there is raised the dreaded spectre of hoax, hyped upon an unsuspecting public. Genuine scientific progress can only be made when all the evidence is openly and honestly examined and not simply a few carefully selected items.

Dinosaurs also present a big problem to the conventional ancient creationist and the specific purpose for their existence so many millions of years ago needs to be identified. On this basis it also is admitted that other creatures and 'peoples' apparently lived a long time ago. The scriptures of course know nothing of such conjectures so that ancient creationists are sometimes described as 'closet evolutionists'.

Perhaps a brief reference to the mammoths buried in the frozen tundra of Canada and Siberia is appropriate at this stage. On a summer day, only a few thousand years ago, many literally froze to death. Quick-freeze experts reckon that the temperature must have suddenly dropped by very many degrees for such an unbelievable event to have happened.

While the actual cause remains a mystery, our attention is drawn to two unique incidents recorded in the Old Testament - in the life of Joshua (Joshua 10:9-14) and during the reign of Hezekiah (Isaiah 38:7-8). The sun was a common factor and it is possible that matters connected with one or other of these events may have precipitated the drastic drop in temperature. King Hezekiah reigned in Judah about 2,700 years ago while Joshua is to be dated around 700 years earlier - in other words, a few thousand years ago !

With regard to Joshua's unique 'long day', there was the specific mention of large hailstones and this was probably linked with a comet depositing super-cooled material. Interestingly, at the time of Joshua, both the Aztecs and the Incas, on the other side of the globe, referred to a day when, for them, the sun never rose - the earth's rotation, tilt or axis was affected - from space! And in the fields of archaeology, geology,astronomy and history, there is abundant evidence to confirm that the earth encountered physical upheavals about three to four thousand years ago which also included the Exodus from Egypt and the formation of the Rift Valley.

Concluding Thoughts

There are two principal views with regard to the age of the earth.

Firstly, it is impossible for the evolutionist to reduce his timescale because, in so doing, he must abandon his belief. Bereft of some billions of years, he automatically retires from the field or else presents a new acceptable theory - there is currently none other available!

To be realistic, his stance has been under intense pressure, as has been often noted in this book. His claim for a lengthy period of time appears to be based on expedience rather than evidence. For example, there is no fossil support for his vital intermediates, the weary struggle to retain the 'uniformitarian' idea has effectively been lost and the Big Bang theory, which is unacceptable to many scientists, actually creates more problems than it solves. Recently the editor of the 'New Scientist' penned: 'never has such a mighty edifice been built on such insubstantial foundations'. In this respect, in an Australian newspaper, a scientist wrote a couple of years ago: 'You have to understand first there is speculation, then there is wild speculation and then there is cosmology !' As evolution is no more than a man-made belief, it is of course possible that it may be abandoned in the future. Accordingly, if it were to be ditched, it is likely that the notion of a Big Bang may become no more than one of many discarded theories.

Perhaps it is the growing evidence that the dinosaur is to be dated more recently which has torpedoed the evolution flagship well below the waterline. When assumed hundreds of millions of years turn out to be some thousands of actual years, the war is really over and the mopping-up process has begun. So beyond credibility is diehard Darwinism that, for example, if genuine dinosaurs were discovered in Congo or China, these findings may have little impact on the belief. There would be some measure of surprise but possibly no change of heart and it is such a system with which the child of God should have no truck whatsoever.

In the second place, there is the belief in special creation whose advocates divide into two main groups. There are those, for example, who stress that, while God created the heavens and the earth at the beginning, he only took action comparatively recently to prepare the earth for our habitation. This view therefore implies that, for some alleged billions of years, the Almighty did not take any action whatsoever in our local arena. More to the point, it requires the Hebrew word 'beginning' (Genesis 1:1) to have a different concept and timescale from a similar Greek word in Matthew 19:4. The problem, previously expressed about evolutionary dating, is equally applicable to the ancient creation viewpoint. Once vast aeons are introduced, the spectre of Darwinism may also be accorded a lease of life which is unwarranted.

Finally, there is the belief in a recent creation. It is of course impossible to be definitive but a time within the last 10,000 to 20,000 years would apparently be acceptable to most creationists. There is little doubt that the plain straightforward reading of the bible and history points to such an approach.

The Kingdom of God has been in the hands of the Christian church for almost 2,000 years and, before that, it was in Jewish hands for a similar period. Peleg and the dramatic happenings in his lifetime are possibly to be dated about 5,000 to 6,000 years ago. The Tower of Babel dispersion perhaps occurred between 6,000 to 8,000 years ago. On this basis, the great deluge in the time of Noah is to be dated within the last 10,000 years.

Some of the above dates are not settled but they do provide a framework based on historical research. In order to place Adam, who was created at the beginning, we are totally dependent on the completeness or otherwise of the Genesis genealogies. The suggested post-Flood dates clearly infer it is impossible to even attempt an approximate date for Adam.

While it is not essential to life to have a date for the age of the earth, it is absolutely vital for eternal life to have a personal relationship with Jesus Christ of Nazareth, the Saviour of the world - there is salvation in no other Name (Acts 4:10-12).

Postscript

As a brief postscript, specific reference requires to be made to the very recent find in Ethiopia of 'Australopithecus ramidus' which is currently dated at

4.5 million years ago by means of the argon method and also by analysis of nearby fossils. Other 'links' have been suggested in the past but these fossils are thought to be nearest to the time, about 6 million years ago, when the human and chimp species allegedly separated.

In the first place, evolutionists once postulated that their common ancestor lived around 20 million years ago. This date has now been dramatically reduced to only 6 million years and no doubt it will be further amended as time goes on. But exactly how and why did this species part and evolve separately? Other remains were found close by and there has been no difficulty in recognising them as antelopes and monkeys. This of course raises the question as to why they did not evolve over the last 4.5 million years! It was none other than Darwin himself who was certain that 'not one living species would transmit its unaltered likeness to a distant futurity'. In the event however this idea is a fallacy as there are many examples of living organisms which have not changed at all during the time since they were fossilised. These are sometimes referred to as 'living fossils'. And of course the fossil record as a whole reveals a most glaring lack of intermediates which is frankly conceded by Darwinists.

Secondly, it is often forgotten that, in the past, there was the extinction of literally hundreds of species. If 'ramidus' were actually a discrete species, can it be conclusively shown it is not around somewhere today? While its extinction cannot be proved, it is also possible to assume that it became extinct before passing on its unique characteristics, however it actually acquired them in the first place. To claim that 'ramidus' was an ancestor is therefore no more than speculation. For one reason, there was nowhere near sufficient time for such an unguided fundamental transformation to have successfully occurred.

Thirdly, there are real difficulties with reference to dating which can only be as good as the various assumptions made. Mind-set plays a key part in this exercise to such an extent that many dates which do not conform are either discarded or adjusted. The world-wide fossil graveyards provide overwhelming evidence of earlier catastrophic events, such as earthquakes, eruptions and floods, rather than slow gradual processes. Dating based on naive uniformitarian ideas is clearly overstated and unreliable and it is also erroneous to use rocks to date fossils and fossils to date rocks, as previously discussed. It thus demands lots of faith to believe that a molar tooth, simply lying among pebbles on the ground, really belonged to a creature that died about 4.5 million years ago!

Fourthly, we need to remember that Neo-Darwinism today, even among leading adherents, is to be regarded as a belief. Without the vital notion of a lengthy timescale, the whole edifice would crumble and rapidly disappear. Sinful human nature, being what it is, will always see what it wishes to see and find what it needs to find! Self-delusion however will not in any way diminish the reality of God's judgment.

In a different but related context, the study of human genes has shown that, for example, we share over 98% of them with chimpanzees. And yet we are clearly separate and unique! Man outstrips any other creature in intelligence and in the use of tools and equipment. Chimps and apes do not reflect on the purpose of life nor are they anxious over global problems. They have never been observed appreciating the beauty of flowers or the wonder of the heavens. They are not religious in any way and yet every human tribe so far discovered has had some form of religion. There is, in fact, an unbridgeable gulf between the primates and ourselves thus confirming that the Creator specially made mankind 'in the image of God'.

Finally, as if to underline the view that dinosaurs and similar creatures ought to be more recently dated, the remains of a 40 ft sea monster were washed up in northern Russia in October 1994. It had apparently fur or feathers and resembled a dinosaur. Indeed some readers may recall that, in 1977, a Japanese fishing boat trawled up the remains of a possible plesiosaur off the coast of South Island, New Zealand. The surprise catch was actually featured on Japanese postage stamps of the time.

It must again be emphasised that the Big Bang is no more than a theory or model. Revised estimates currently indicate a figure of 8 billion years for the age of the universe, a staggering 50% drop from that previously believed. Fossil and historical records however loudly proclaim the message of catastrophism and thus insist that the earth is much younger than evolutionary theory suggests. The Word of God teaches that, rather than an assumed gradual expansion, the universe actually sprang into existence at the beginning.

Appendix III

Message from Atlantis

Due to the perverse indoctrination of Darwinism, many simply imagine that human beings evolved from apes a long time ago. We are told about primitive peoples and yet we also learn about great and powerful communities stretching back, it seems, to the dawn of civilisation. It all can be very confusing and even the experts in antiquities refer to mysteries and problems which appear to be insoluble at this stage.

Many difficulties would however be removed if only we would get back to the Word of God and this has been the burden and thrust of this particular book. We need to remember that God created a perfect world with people of real ability to seek to understand and to master what he had provided (Genesis 1:28).

Genesis however narrates that Adam and Eve overstepped the mark in a vain attempt to become as 'gods' themselves. Nevertheless, as previously discussed, there was a growth in knowledge and know-how and, when such technique was coupled with longevity of life, the potential for expertise and sophistication was basically unlimited. This varied development was recorded in the early chapters of Genesis and it specifically included the ability, over many years, to construct an ark of gigantic proportions.

After the year of the catastrophic worldwide Flood, Noah, his family and the animals were commanded and enabled to re-populate the earth. In Noah and his sons, there was of course an abundance of age and experience which we cannot even begin to comprehend. This knowledge was naturally handed down to their families and descendants and in Genesis chapter 11 we notice their staggering ability to build a city and a tower (of Babel) on such a scale that it appeared as if the tower could even reach into heaven itself!

The Almighty however purposed to scatter the inhabitants over all the earth. This dispersion took place with different groups taking more or less knowledge and skills with them in much the same way as has been happening in history ever since. It is at this stage, as the chapter title suggests, that we have to link this scenario with some consideration as to how events probably developed.

There were two well known civilisations in the Middle East about the time of the fourth millennium before Christ - Egypt and Sumer. They were based around the river Nile and the river Euphrates respectively and experts are certain that they actually developed independently. There is however the vital discovery that both civilisations made exceptional progress in a rather brief period of time. This has prompted the concept of 'Atlantis' (not the Atlantic!) which is referred to in ancient literature. Atlantis was understood to have been an advanced civilisation whose territory became covered by water. Those escaping by boat made their way to Egypt and Sumer, thus explaining the extraordinary development in these cultures.

While it is impossible to identify the exact location of Atlantis, some researchers would place it in the general area of Arabia and the Arabian Sea. It is however very likely to have been a territory which was equidistant from the Nile Delta and the Lower Euphrates. Apparently, after the dispersion from Babel, some of the community with well advanced techniques held together while others spread out far and wide on the earth. They, of Atlantis, knew only too well of the great deluge in the time of their ancestor Noah and so, in their particular locality, they had boats in readiness in case the need arose in the future. In the event, there was at least one other flood (or tidal wave) with devastating consequences but from which many, if not all, were able to escape and finally make their way to Egypt and Sumer. (The people from Atlantis may be referred to as 'The Civilisers' or 'The Dynastic Race').

We must now note some interesting facts about these early civilisations. The Hanging Gardens of Babylon and the Egyptian pyramids were among the seven wonders of the ancient world. A top archaeologist described the achievement in respect of the pyramids: 'it is to be compared with the finest opticians' work on a scale of acres'. Undoubtedly the skills and organisational ability of that culture have been irretrievably lost today. This was evidenced when, some years ago, a team of Japanese engineers tried to build a 35 feet high replica of the Great Pyramid (the original was over 481 feet in height!). They failed using only the techniques proved by archaeology and they also gave up even after bringing the necessary modern equipment onto the site.

Our story now enters a very important stage. Years ago, archaeologists discovered a cedarwood boat buried and dismantled in a pit beside the Great Pyramid at Giza. This was a giant vessel, more than 142 feet in length, and it has been apparently dated about 4,500 years ago. (Other boat pits were also found). These have puzzled the Egyptologists and the orthodox assumption has been that all boats were required for some religious purpose relating to the afterlife of the kings.

It would now seem that this conjecture may be incorrect. Centuries earlier, 'the men from Atlantis' had escaped a flood or whatever by means of boats and finally came to Egypt. They had, in their possession, stores of knowledge and expertise which effectively transformed Egypt overnight. While they had escaped from a watery grave, they ensured, by passing on the details, that their descendants would not perish in the event of another flood(s). Hence the provision of substantial boats which could ride out breakers and even the high seas.

It therefore appears that the above scenario is likely to be the explanation of what has long puzzled the Egyptologists. In this light, we may also have the answer to that intriguing name in Genesis 10:25 - the name of Peleg which refers to division or separation and, in its root meaning, is invariably linked with water, for example, Isaiah 30:25 and Job 38:25. It is probable that, when the earth was 'divided' in Peleg's time, the reference was not to the splitting-up of the world's population after the tower of Babel event. This dispersion had already taken place, as we have discussed. The Peleg episode is directly linked with water in the form of sea flooding (or tidal waves) affecting many areas of the Middle East and no doubt much farther afield. It is more than likely that this was not an isolated incident and that such events occurred during Peleg's lifetime and afterwards. (Peleg only lived for 239 years while his 'father' Eber - from whom the word 'Hebrews' is derived - lived for 464 years. This large drop in longevity is possibly another indicator that the word 'father' may occasionally mean 'ancestor' in Genesis chapters 10 and 11 and thus makes dating rather uncertain).

We now face the inevitable questions - what caused the earth division by water in Peleg's time and also submerged ancient Atlantis? The prime factor was presumably the Noachic flood of judgment which of course occurred much earlier. This however had a devastating impact on the earth, the repercussions of which were felt over a lengthy period, giving rise to the opening up of the land mass. At that time,the waters generally invaded the lands but without overwhelming them, as occurred in the days of Noah, and it was this type of event which basically caused the fossil graveyards around the earth. (The Noachic flood had earlier swept away, with possibly little trace, all that were outside the ark - Matthew 24:39). Further reference to the widespread upheavals on the earth a few thousand years ago is also relevant with regard to fossil finds and rock strata.

The earth is still recovering from past happenings

which included the ice and the snow. Inland seas and lakes have been steadily drying up and there has been the noticeable spread of desert areas.

In general, many of the matters considered in this chapter have clear links with the bible and they are probably to be dated within the last 10,000 years. Geologists will be familiar with some of these concepts but, because of their fatal obsession with the idea of uniformitarianism, many date these events millions of years ago. In so doing, they deliberately ignore, and thus cause others to ignore, the explicit details of a past judgment by God and a certain day of future judgment and destruction (2 Peter 3: 3-13). The Day of the Lord will certainly come 'as a thief' and it behoves each one of us to be ready - now ! God made mankind 'in his own image', primarily to be 'spirit', and hence physical death can never mean the end for any individual - 'after death the judgment' (Hebrews 9:27-28).

In the scriptures God has revealed matters of which mankind would be totally unaware, events which must be taken into account to obtain a genuine understanding of past history. There was a special creation. There was a universal Flood and later happenings over succeeding millennia including the onset and impact of the Ice Age.

It is generally accepted that very cold winters followed by hot summers do not produce an Ice Age. There are numerous theories about such an occurrence but essential ingredients include warmer winters, abundant snowfall and cooler summers. This type of scenario apparently developed from the Flood. Sea and ocean levels also fell as waters turned to ice thus providing various land-bridges to assist in the widespread freedom of movement. Some scientists from different disciplines insist that the major Ice Age in early human history was a unique event because such conditions will not again prevail on the earth. In other words, there will never be another worldwide Flood which of course accords with the Word of God (Genesis 9:11-17).

Concentrating on the position today, several climatologists are of the firm belief that we have already entered the so-called 'Greenhouse Century', which, to an extent, is of our own making. Relatively small increases in average temperatures are expected to create really difficult environmental situations around the world. However, as acceptance of the evolution hypothesis is so prevalent, it is thought that these problems may well be smoothed out naturally.

Should this hypothesis be flawed, as discussed elsewhere, the outlook is very serious indeed. This is because what is assumed to have been safely negotiated on a previous occasion(s) did not genuinely occur and thus the grim reckoning may be faced next century and that for the first time. (The anticipated growth in world population will also bring increased difficulties. To compound this situation, scientists have recently detected a comet which may possibly collide with planet earth during the coming decades. Bearing in mind the crash of the Shoemaker-Levy comet into Jupiter in July 1994, the potential of such a collision or near collision would be catastrophic, reminiscent of the global events which occurred three or four thousand years ago. It is of course a moot point whether all the flood traditions refer to such happenings or to the earlier Noachic deluge).

The whole of creation has been groaning in pain from the Fall. Sooner or later God's judgment will be meted out no matter what unbelieving people may imagine. What we witness today will be no more. The Almighty will usher in a new heaven and earth for the old order of things will have passed away (Revelation 21:1-4). 'Time' will actually have run out!

Further Reading

The Word of God
Scofield Reference Bible
The Life and Teaching of Jesus Christ: James S. Stewart
The Millennium: Loraine Boettner
COSMOLOGY:
In the Beginning: John Gribbin
EVOLUTION:
The Blind Watchmaker: Richard Dawkins
Growing Up in the Universe: Richard Dawkins (Royal Institution 1991 Christmas Lectures)
The Making of Mankind: Richard Leakey
The Facts of Life: (critical) Richard Milton
Darwin on Trial: (critical) Phillip E. Johnson
Bones of Contention: (critical) Marvin Lubenow
Evolution: A Theory in Crisis: (critical) Michael Denton
THEISTIC EVOLUTION:
Genesis Today: Ernest V. Lucas
CREATION (ANCIENT):
Creation and Evolution: Alan Hayward
CREATION (RECENT):
Astronomy and the Bible: Donald B. De Young
Creation Science: David Rosevear